Making  HAPPY

THE ART AND SCIENCE OF A HAPPY MARRIAGE

Drs. Les & Leslie Parrott

#1 *New York Times* Best-Selling Authors

WORTHY

PUBLISHING

Library of Congress Control Number: 2013954260

For foreign and subsidiary rights, contact Rights@WorthyPublishing.com

Published in association with Yates & Yates, yates2.com

ISBN: 978-1-61795-326-2 (trade paper)

Cover Design: Brandon Hill Design
Interior Design and Typesetting: Hudson & Associates

Printed in the United States of America
15 16 17 18 19 lbm 9 8 7 6 5 4 3 2

Making
HAPPY

To Corey and Mia Hays.
One of the happiest couples we know.
And a couple who has brought
unending happiness into our family.

- Do you know what you can do to instantly make your relationship 25 percent happier—starting today?

- Do you know how to counter the inevitable effects of taking each other for granted?

- Are you using happiness to build a firewall of protection around your relationship?

- Do you know the easy way to ensure that your partner is happier today than yesterday?

- Are you avoiding the most common mistake couples make in pursuing happiness together?

- Did you think marriage would make you happy—instead of you making your marriage happy?

- Are you ready to deepen your relationship by being happy in love?

Making Happy
reveals the answer to these questions and more!

Making HAPPY

Contents

PART THREE
C'mon,
Get Happy!

"The highest happiness on earth is the happiness of marriage."
William Lyon Phelps

Hooked on a Feeling

Knowledge of what is possible
is the beginning of happiness.

George Santayana

YOU MAY NOT KNOW his name, but Jason McElwain made a lot of people happy. As a struggling autistic high school student in Rochester, New York, he was a long way from making the cut for the school's basketball team. But his heart was in the sport, so the coach let him help out as "team manager." Jason took the job seriously and his fellow classmates respected him for it. He even wore a white shirt and black tie to every game as he sat on the end of bench, fetching towels and water for the players.

In his senior year the coach did something unexpected. He put Jason into the game with four minutes and nineteen seconds left on the clock. The crowd in that high school gym went wild, cheering Jason's name.

Jason took his first shot—missing the hoop by about six feet. But one minute later he got the ball again and made a three-pointer that set the gym on fire.

Jason wasn't done. He kept shooting and kept hitting. He scored twenty points in four minutes during his one and only game. He made six three-pointers—a school record.

In the news clip, Coach Johnson got choked up retelling Jason's story. "In twenty-five years of coaching I've never experienced the emotional high of that game," he said. "I just started to cry." And he's not the only one. The clip spread like wildfire through social media with more than three million hits and comments like:

"Oh no, I'm crying at work!"

"Amazing. I'm Facebooking this now."

"Just what I needed. Thanks!"

Teary joy wells up in almost everyone who sees the elated home crowd storming the court after Jason's final three-pointer and lifting him on their shoulders. Why? Because you can't help but to get an emotional lift yourself. The happy pandemonium in the gym is contagious. You want to share it with others.

We've shown the clip to students in our university classes, many who have seen it before, and they literally cheer and applaud the screen. When asked to describe their feelings we hear words like *awe, delight, thrill, surprise.* But mostly we hear *happy.*

The human spirit hungers to be borne aloft. We want a nudge toward happiness. Our God-given capacity for uplift is what makes us euphorically human. And according to a growing mountain of scientific research, happiness is not only critical to our relationships and well-being, it doesn't depend on the uncommon McElwain brand of exhilaration hitting our e-mail's in-box.

Lifting our spirits, thankfully, isn't contingent upon finding YouTube miracles like Jason's basketball experience, Susan Boyle's surprisingly stunning solo on *Britain's Got Talent*, or "Sully" Sullenberger's phenomenal airline landing on the Hudson River. And our happiness—the kind that endures—certainly doesn't depend on getting a job promotion or winning the lottery. In fact, most of the things we think will make us happier don't. Humans, it turns out, are extraordinarily bad at predicting their own happiness (more on that later).

Isn't Marriage Supposed to Make Us Happy?

One of the most pervasive happiness myths is the notion that when we find our perfect partner—when we say "I do"—we'll have a lock on happiness. And we will, for a time. No doubt about it: marriage makes us happy. The problem is that marriage—even when initially perfectly satisfying—will not make us intensely happy for as long as we believe it will. Studies reveal that the happiness boost from marriage lasts an average of only two years.[1]

Unfortunately, when those two years are up and fulfilling our goal to find the ideal partner hasn't made us as happy as we expected, we often feel there must be something wrong with us or we must be the only ones to feel this way. But we're not. It's the common course of love. And if left unattended, if we're not deliberately making happy together, our relationship suffers. If we turn the right dials to boost our happiness factor in love, however, our relationship soars.

Happiness, for a marriage, is like a vital sign. It's the heart rate of love. Like all vital signs, it can fluctuate. But, like all vital signs, it has a set point, a level to which it strives to return. For healthy couples doing the right things, that set point is high. And when done well, marriage is a better predictor of happiness than having money or children.

This book, *Making Happy*, is dedicated to helping you keep the vital sign of happiness healthy and strong in your relationship. How will we do this? Not with armchair psychology. The strategies and principles of this book are built on an incredible amount of solid, time-tested research.

The New Science of Happiology

Psychologists have always been interested in emotion, but in the past two decades the studies have exploded, and one of the emotions that psychologists have studied most intensively is happiness—a topic that was previously in the exclusive hands of philosophers and poets. Even economists and neuroscientists have joined the happiness party. All these disciplines have distinct but intersecting interests: psychologists want to understand how people feel happy, economists want to know the value of happiness, and neuroscientists want to know how people's brains process and produce happiness.

Having three separate disciplines all interested in a single subject has put that topic on the scientific map. Papers on happiness are now published in the most prestigious peer-reviewed journals, scholars who study happiness are winning Nobel Prizes, and even governments around the world are rushing to measure and increase the happiness of their citizens.

Happiness is one of life's most cherished goals. On every continent, in every country, and in every culture, when people are asked,

"What do you want?" the most popular answer is "happiness." When parents are asked, "What do you most want for your children?" the answer is most often "happiness."

And when couples are asked about the kind of relationship they most want, they'll talk about being happy together. "The happy state of matrimony," said Benjamin Franklin, "is the surest and most lasting foundation of comfort and love." Oliver Wendell Homes added: "Love is the master key that opens the gates of happiness."

Making Happy Together

No doubt about it, love and happiness make beautiful music together. But truth be told, happiness is in short supply for too many time-starved and sleep-deprived couples. And the reason, we suspect, is that they don't work at it—or more likely, they don't know *how* to make it. Happiness, after all, is not something that *happens*, it's something you *make*.

Some even call it quits for this very reason, saying: "We're just not happy anymore." Really? Is being married supposed to make you happy? No. That's not how it works. Marriage doesn't make *you* happy—you make your *marriage* happy. As the saying goes, you bring your own weather to the picnic. A happy marriage does not depend on the right circumstances or the perfect person. A happy marriage is the result of two people committed to making a happy life of love together.[2]

Every once in a while we encounter someone who tries to argue that making happy is a selfish pursuit. We understand that thought. After all, some silly and downright selfish things are done in the name of pursing happiness. Many a marriage counselor will attest to hearing something along these lines: "I'm not happy in this marriage; God wants me to be happy; therefore I want out of this marriage." This self-centered perspective is mistaking hedonism for happiness. They think their circumstances are supposed to make them happy. They are pursuing pleasure at the cost of meaning. Don't fall for this lie. Hedonism does not equal happiness. Hedonism, the goal of which is to maximize net pleasure, lacks *meaning* altogether. And meaning, as you'll see in Part One of this book, is a vitally important ingredient of true happiness. It's a fact, not just a biblical sentiment: You'll find more happiness in giving yourself away than in any self-centered pleasure.

Our long-time friend Gary Thomas, author of *Sacred Marriage* and many other books, is well-known for asking this question: "What if God designed marriage to make us holy instead of happy?" How could it be otherwise? The pursuit of holiness can't help but bring an abiding happiness and joy. Why? Because holiness, being devoted to God's ways of being, subsumes *meaning* and *love*. And true happiness is never fulfilled without it. When we sow holiness, we reap happiness.

Truth be told, happy people are more loving people—the very opposite of selfish. When we get a lock on true happiness, it makes us more sociable and self-giving; it increases how much we like ourselves and our partner. Happiness improves our ability to resolve conflict. The bottom line: happiness makes us more loving and lovable. That, in a nutshell, is why we wrote this book.

What This Book Will Do for You

Why write a book on happiness and love? Because emerging research from neuroscience and psychology makes the link between a thriving relationship and certain happy behaviors absolutely clear.

We've learned a lot about what makes couples happy, and we've put the principles to work in our own marriage—and we'd be stupid not to use that knowledge.

That's why this book is nothing if not practical. We have combed through all the scientific studies we could find on happiness to lift out the best of what we know works to make and maintain happiness in marriage. And we've settled on a half dozen *happiness boosters* that are sure to move the needle in your relationship. These are the six dials we know couples can turn to get the best effects:

- *Count your blessings*—nothing can increase happiness more quickly in a relationship than shared gratitude.
- *Try new things*—it's easy to fall into a routine or even a rut, but that is a killer to happiness, so you've got to shake it up.
- *Dream a dream*—the moment a couple quits looking to the future together is the moment they become vulnerable to dissatisfaction.
- *Celebrate each other*—we all applaud the big things, but it's the little and unexpected celebrations that can make or break a couple's happiness.
- *Attune your spirits*—the soul of every marriage hungers for deeper connection and meaning together, and when it's found, happiness abounds.
- *Add value to others*—when a couple does good beyond the boundaries of their marriage, goodness envelopes their relationship like never before.

These are the six boosters we'll explore with you, giving you dozens of practical ways to bring each of them more fully into your relationship. And we want to say this straight out: this book is not about making changes that involve more time, energy, or money. Making happiness is in many ways easier than you think.

We want this book to be interactive for the two of you (and even with other couples if you're using it in a small group). That's why we've provided you with questions at the end of each chapter. We hope you'll take time to use them together. By discussing, not just reading, the book with each other, the content will become far more personal and it will sink deeper roots into your relationship.

In the last section of the book you'll see that we've also provided you with a Three-Week Happiness Plan. We literally provide you with a little assignment for each of the twenty-one days in this plan. They are proven to work. We have done them ourselves and so have countless couples we've taught them to. You will love this plan. It is sure to infuse your marriage with deeper joy and more happiness. In short, it will guarantee that the two of you make more happy together.

Our Hope and Prayer for You

We've written every word of this book with you in mind. We want you to discover a deep and abiding joy in your relationship. We want you to make happy like you never have before. Why? Because you simply can't take a happy marriage for granted. Under normal circumstances, despite what you think, you will not live happily ever after. We all know the staggering divorce statistics. But have you ever considered all the couples who stay together in a dissatisfied and unhappy marriage? One of the most consistent findings in marriage research reveals that marital satisfaction declines over the course of marriage. Many couples grow accustomed to feeling despondent, cranky, and increasingly dissatisfied in their relationship—and they do nothing about it. And too often relatively happy couples don't know how to move from feeling good to feeling great in their relationship.

So remember this as you begin this book: marriage cannot be counted on to make you happy. You *make* your happiness in marriage. Unless you are *making* happy, the relationship you counted on to make you happy is likely to leave you feeling empty. But when you make happy together you are building a healthy hedge of protection around your love. Your marriage will not only go the distance, it will put a huge smile on each of your faces.

Les and Leslie Parrott
Seattle, Washington

PART ONE

The Happiness Advantage for Couples

1 Let the Happiness Begin

Happiness isn't a mood. It's a way of life.

Noel Smogard

THE LIST OF FAMOUS students from the hallowed halls of Harvard University is long, to be sure: John Hancock, Ralph Waldo Emerson, Helen Keller, Leonard Bernstein, John F. Kennedy, George W. Bush, Barack Obama, and Mark Zuckerberg, to name just a few. It makes sense. After all, the school has a long history. And as the oldest institution of higher education in the United States, founded in 1636, Harvard is pretty entrenched in convention and tradition. But not as much as you might guess.

Beginning in 2006, two professors, Tal Ben-Shahar and Shawn Achor, offered an unconventional course that remains the most popular class on campus, with an attendance of about fifteen hundred students per semester. No course has ever commanded such numbers at Harvard. Not before or since.

Professor Achor admits that he and Ben-Shahar have been shocked by its popularity. They never dreamed so many students would be interested in what they are teaching: *happiness*. But they are.

> The greater part of our happiness or misery depends upon our dispositions, and not upon our circumstances.
> *Martha Washington*

The Science of Happiness, the official course title, is often dubbed Happiness 101, and as the course syllabus says, it focuses on "aspects of a fulfilling and flourishing life." Remember, this is Harvard University—the school known for its high academic standards and rigorous requirements. How could such a course on such a squishy topic be taken seriously?

Getting Serious about Happiness

Hearing that Harvard was offering a course on happiness caused some scholars at other august institutions around the country to raise an eyebrow or two. Some skeptics believed it was a hoax. When Tal Ben-Shahar appeared as a guest on Comedy Central's *The Daily Show with Jon Stewart*, Stewart asked how he could "get away" with a scholarly school having a course on such a soft and fuzzy subject. Ben-Shahar answered, "We now have a science of happiness."[1]

And we do. The word *science* is right there in the course title. But it's more than semantics. The number of scholarly studies on happiness has exploded over the past two decades. Until recently, the countless studies produced by social scientists had been directed toward the other end of the human experience continuum—anxiety, depression, neurosis, obsessions, paranoia, delusions, and depression.

Why? It all started about one hundred years ago with a doctor in Vienna, Austria.

Paging Dr. Freud

Sigmund Freud, the father of psychoanalysis, wasn't a happy camper. He saw human beings as troubled creatures in need of repair. Freud himself was profoundly pessimistic about human nature, saying we are governed by deep, dark drives that we can barely control.

B. F. Skinner and the behaviorists who followed Freud weren't much happier, viewing human life as mechanistic if not robotic: humans were passive beings mercilessly shaped by stimuli and rewards or punishments.

In fact, some of psychology's most well-known experiments proved that normal people could become coldly insensitive to suffering and even cruelly sadistic. Research funders invested in subjects like *conformity*, *neurosis*, and *depression*.

The Comprehensive Textbook of Psychiatry, the expensive clinical bible of psychiatry, has five hundred thousand lines of text. There are thousands of lines on anxiety and depression and hundreds of lines on terror, shame, guilt, anger, and fear. But there are only five lines on hope, one line on joy, and not a single line on compassion, creativity, forgiveness, laughter, or

> The great Western disease is, 'I'll be happy when . . . When I get the money. When I get a BMW. When I get this job.' Well, the reality is, you never get to when. The only way to find happiness is to understand that happiness is not out there. It's in here. And happiness is not next week. It's now.
>
> *Marshall Goldsmith*

love. You get the idea. From the beginning and for nearly a century, social scientists have had little to say about positive virtues. But not anymore. Something happened in 1998 that changed everything.

O Happy Day!

When University of Pennsylvania psychologist Martin Seligman was elected president of the American Psychological Association by the largest vote in the organization's history, he gave a powerful keynote address to his fellow psychologists. On a balmy October night in North Carolina, his message was clear and blunt: he wanted psychologists to expand their myopic focus on treating mental illness and include promoting mental health. The same month, in the organization's newsletter, he wrote a piece titled "Building Human Strength: Psychology's Forgotten Mission," and said: "Psychology is not just the study of weakness and damage, it is also the study of strength and virtue. Treatment is not just fixing what is broken, it is nurturing what is best within ourselves."[2] No doubt about it, Seligman wanted nothing short of a new day, a sea change, a transformation or even a revolution of his profession. And he got it.

> My happiness grows in direct proportion to my acceptance, and in inverse proportion to my expectations.
>
> *Michael J. Fox*

Seligman's speech and the work that followed launched a new movement among social scientists that is now known as Positive Psychology.[3] As evidence, you'll find scientific journals dedicated to it, massive funding, countless studies, and hundreds of courses like the one on happiness at Harvard. Pathology, of course, still garners plenty of grant money and research, but a new wave of science has shed an amazing amount of light on the positive virtues and character qualities most humans aspire to.[4]

Before going too much further, however, let's make sure we know what we're talking about when we say *happiness*.

Happiness Defined

Serious exploration of happiness isn't new, of course. Classical thinkers like Socrates, Plato, and Aristotle gave plenty of attention to it. And every language, without exception, going back to ancient Greek, has a word for *happiness*. But while we use the same word, we often don't mean the same thing.

> Success is getting what you want, happiness is wanting what you get.
>
> *W. P. Kinsella*

People prior to the late seventeenth century thought happiness was a matter of luck or divine favor. Even the root of *happiness, hap*, means "chance." Happiness was not something you could control. It was dictated by fate or fortune. Happiness literally happened to us and was out of our hands.

Today we think of happiness more as a skill that can be developed. The founding fathers of the United Stated, in fact, made clear that happiness was a right to be *pursued*. This new way of thinking engendered more noble humanitarian sentiments—the belief that suffering is inherently wrong and that all people, in all places, should have the opportunity to be happy.

But this new way of thinking about happiness also comes with a challenge. When happiness becomes a given *right*, it backs away from being something won through moral cultivation, carried out over the course of a well-lived life. Instead, it runs the risk of becoming something "out there" that is not only pursued, but also caught and consumed. And that's where the pursuit of happiness can cause problems.[5]

> Happiness is not in our circumstance but in ourselves. It is not something we see, like a rainbow, or feel, like the heat of a fire. Happiness is something we are.
>
> *John B. Sheerin*

Before we delineate happiness further, let's pause for a moment and ask: What is *your* definition of a happy life? Are you living it? Think carefully about this because your definition of *happiness* will influence every other significant decision you make. That may sound like an overstatement, but your definition of *happiness* really does frame your approach to living. If you think happiness is outside you, for example, you will make happiness into a search or a reward to discover or earn. If, however, you know happiness is inside you, then happiness becomes more of a compass, enabling you to live a better life.

These two basic perspectives are not so much the definition of *happiness* as they are the means to finding it. So let's make the definition easy. Ready?

Happiness is the emotional state of feeling satisfaction, playfulness, contentedness, amusement, cheeriness, serenity, gratification, elation, triumph, joy, and/or bliss.

It's important to note that *happiness*, in this definition, is a state. That means it's not static. In other words, even the happiest of people—the cheeriest 10 percent—feel blue at times. And even the bluest have their moments of joy. Like all feelings, happiness can ebb and flow.

There you have it: a straightforward, if not informal, definition of *happiness*. But let's dig deeper. Why? Because happiness—the kind that embodies deep joy—is more than a feeling. To really get to the underlying meaning of *happiness*, you've got to not only pinpoint the feeling but also where it comes from. Why? Because the source of your happiness can make or break your personal pursuit of it.

The Two Wells of Happiness

When someone asked Eleanor Roosevelt to define *happiness*, here's what she said: "A feeling that you have been honest with yourself and those around you; a feeling that you have done the best you could both in your personal life and in your work; and the ability to love others." Mrs. Roosevelt obviously understood happiness to be an inside job.

Researchers call that *intrinsic* happiness because it's values-based. It's the result of personal growth, healthy relationships, contributing to the common good. *Extrinsic* happiness, on the other hand, is feelings based and comes about from obtaining rewards, praise, money, status, or popularity.

Harvard social psychologist William McDougall said people can be happy while in pain and unhappy while experiencing pleasure. Take a moment to let that sink in. You can only be happy in pain when it's values-based. And you can only be unhappy while experiencing pleasure when it's feelings-based. We're really talking about two kinds of happiness that both result in feelings of

> The gap between our professed values and our practiced values is the gap between us and our happiness.
> *Marc Gafni*

satisfaction, gratification, and all the rest, but that have very different levels of shelf life.

Feel-good happiness is the momentary sensation of pleasure. When we joke around or have sex, we experience feel-good happiness. But here's the catch: we know from research that feel-good happiness is ruled by the law of diminishing returns. This type of happiness can lose its punch and it rarely lasts longer than a few hours at a time.

Value-based happiness is a deeper sense that our lives have meaning and fulfill a larger purpose than just pleasure. It represents a spiritual source of satisfaction. And here's some good news: it's not ruled by the law of diminishing returns. This means there's no limit to how meaningful and happy our lives can be. Some like to call values-based happiness *joy* because it's deep and more abiding. That's fine with us. Whatever you call it, it's found in our values.

Value-based happiness is the great equalizer in life. You can find value-based happiness if you are rich or poor, smart or mentally challenged, athletic or clumsy, popular or socially awkward. Wealthy people are not necessarily happy, and poor people are not necessarily unhappy. Values, more than pleasure, provide a deeper well for true happiness, and it's a well everyone can drink from. After all, everybody has the potential to live in accordance with his or her values.

How to Increase Your Odds of Disappointment

Happiness has increasingly been thought to be more about getting little infusions of pleasure, about feeling good rather than being good. For the uninformed, happiness becomes less about a well-lived life and more about experiencing the well-felt moment. That's a dead end to true and solid happiness.

When feel-good happiness becomes more important than value-based happiness, hedonism rears its head. And narcissism isn't far behind. Feeling good becomes the ultimate goal. Toughing it out and self-sacrifice are avoided at all costs. Self-seeking indulgence becomes the name of the game. Their orientation toward external sources of happiness means they're looking for things like admiration, acquiring stuff, and status. And we know from research that people who lean into this kind of happiness report less satisfaction and feel less energized.

> Happiness doesn't depend on what we have, but it does depend on how we feel toward what we have. We can be happy with little and miserable with much.
>
> *William Dempster Hoard*

It's known as the *hedonistic paradox*: when one aims solely towards pleasure itself, one's aim is continually frustrated. That's what novelist Edith Wharton was getting at when she said: "If we'd stop trying to be happy we could have a pretty good time." It's also what underlies what the great teacher Helen Keller said: "True happiness is not attained through gratification, but through a worthy purpose."

Of course, if you swing back the other direction too far and try to avoid feel-good happiness altogether, you risk becoming a stoic or puritan who relies on duty and represses pleasure to prove you can endure without having fun. And who wants that—especially in marriage? Either way, if you embrace one form of happiness exclusively, you instantly increase the odds for being disappointed.

Healthy happiness involves balance. That's why at the heart of this book you'll find a half dozen proven happiness boosters for couples that intermingle both feel-good and value-based happiness. They include things like counting your blessings, trying new things, attuning your spirits, and so on. While some may appear to be exclusive to one camp or the other, they're not. For married couples, these actions are not one-off tricks or techniques to conjure contentment. They are not mere mood managers. They are a way of life. Scratch that. They are a way of being happy in love together.

This Is Your Brain on Happiness

At the base of your brain is a bundle of nerves that wander throughout your body, linking your heart, lungs, and stomach as well as your facial and vocal muscles. The nerve bundle is known as the vagus nerve. It comes from a Latin word that literally means "wandering" (think *vagabond*). Your vagus nerve reduces your heart rate and blood pressure while quietly communicating with the muscles that control respiration and digestion. It's a messenger to your brain saying everything is all right.[6] It's closely associated with oxytocin, the all-important hormone of human trust and devotion.

> It is pleasing to God whenever thou rejoicest or laughest from the bottom of thy heart.
>
> *Martin Luther*

Oxytocin is essential to happiness, according to Jon Haidt, professor at the University of Virginia. In his view, human happiness derives neither from external validation nor solely from within, but from *between*—through the relationships created by love and "something larger than yourself"—whether it's a religious group, a volunteer organization, or a political campaign. "If happiness comes from between," Haidt says, "then oxytocin is the hormone of between. It's the catalyst that helps bond people together."[7]

Oxytocin, often referred to as the love hormone, makes us more sympathetic, supportive, and open with our feelings—all necessary for couples to be happy in love. Studies at Claremont Graduate University have shown that high-oxytocin couples finish each other's sentences, laugh together, and touch each other more often.[8]

> Puritanism is the haunting fear that someone, somewhere, may be happy.
>
> *H. L. Mencken*

The chemicals in our body make us easier to love and be loved. And they are inextricably linked with feeling happy.[9] It's no exaggeration to say we're designed to be happy in love. Of course we don't always hang our happiness on the right actions. That's what this book is about. But make no mistake, you're built to be happy and so is your marriage.

Easy to Live With

Some people are afraid to value happiness. It's true. They think it's selfish. Until the eighteenth century, Western standards encouraged, if anything, a slightly saddened approach to life, with facial expressions to match. Walk through any historical portrait gallery to see what we mean—including the ambivalent smile of a Mona Lisa. Back in the day, good Protestants "allowed no joy or pleasure, but a kind of melancholic demeanor and austerity." [10] They felt it best for sinful humanity to display a somewhat sorrowful humility.

Do you think that's what God wants? We agree with Catherine Marshall who asked: "Whence comes this idea that if what we are doing is fun, it can't be God's will? The God who made giraffes, a baby's fingernails, a puppy's tail, a crooknecked squash, the bobwhite's call, and a young girl's giggle, has a sense of humor. Make no mistake about that." [11]

> No one can live without delight, and that is why a man deprived of spiritual joy goes over to carnal pleasures.
>
> *Thomas Aquinas*

Even Jesus said, "I've told you these things for a purpose: that my joy might be your joy, and your joy wholly mature." [12]

Still, some sincere people, even today, have a tough time valuing happiness because they think it's selfish. But isn't the opposite really true? Isn't unhappiness the ultimate form of self-indulgence? When you're unhappy, you tend to be self-consumed. You take yourself pretty seriously. Happy people, on the other hand are more selfless. When we choose to value happiness, gratitude, playfulness, and joy, we become easy to live with. If this sentiment doesn't sit so well with you, if you're holding onto the idea that happiness is selfish, hang in there with us. We're going to shed more light on this in the next chapter when we expose the "hat trick of happiness."

This book is dedicated to helping you be happy in love together. Does that mean the proverbial fairytale of living happily ever after? We'll get to that. For now it means being easy to live with. And that makes every couple happy.

For Reflection

1. Why do you think it took social scientists so long to begin studying happiness and well-being?
2. What do you make of the two wells of happiness: feel-good happiness and value-based happiness? Do you agree that value-based happiness is the great equalizer in life? Why or why not?
3. Are you easy to live with? Why or why not? And if you increased your level of happiness, do you think it would make you easier to live with? How so?

2 Do You Know Your Happy Factor?

There are only two tragedies in life: one is not getting what one wants, and the other is getting it.

Oscar Wilde

WHEN STEPHEN AND TERRI Weaver set out for a daylong fishing trip, they had no idea they would come back millionaires.

Sixty miles northeast of Little Rock, Arkansas, the couple stopped at a convenience store and picked up a lottery ticket on their way to a fishing spot. They stopped at the same store again on their way home and decided to grab another lottery ticket.

The couple won big that day in 2013—not once, but twice. The first ticket the Weavers purchased netted the couple a one-million-dollar prize, while the second ticket put a cherry on top with another fifty thousand dollars.

Kind of makes you think twice about going fishing together, doesn't it? After all, what couple wouldn't like to suddenly have a million dollars show up in their bank account?

But many lottery winners find their pot of gold brings loss. In 1997 a man named Billie Bob Harrell and his wife, Barbara Jean, won thirty-one million dollars in the Texas lottery. With three children to support, the first of their $1.24-million annual payouts seemed like the light at the end of the tunnel. Instead it was the beginning of a horrifying year for the couple. It started out joyful: he quit his job at Home Depot and they took a trip to Hawaii, donated tens of thousands of dollars to their church, bought cars and houses for friends and family, and even donated 480 turkeys to the poor.

> If more of us valued food and cheer and song above hoarded gold, it would be a merrier world.
>
> *J. R. R. Tolkien*

But the spending and lending spiraled out of control. Just months after winning the jackpot tensions splintered their marriage. They separated. And tragically, twenty months after winning the lottery, Harrell committed suicide. Shortly before his death he told a financial adviser: "Winning the lottery is the worst thing that ever happened to me."

It's not an isolated story. Numerous big-money winners end up regretting the win they longed for. Not only does more money not make them happier, it often makes them flat-out miserable.

Mo' Money, Mo' Happy?

We can almost hear you saying, "Well, I wouldn't mind having to struggle to be happier with a few extra million dollars in my bank account." Okay. We hear that. But beware. A landmark study on happiness and major lottery winners published in the *Journal of Personality and Social Psychology* found that the overall happiness levels of lottery winners spiked when they won but returned to prewinning levels after just a few months. In terms of overall happiness, the lottery winners were no more happy than the nonwinners and were sometimes less happy than they were before winning.[1]

Another study at the University of California, Santa Barbara measured people's happiness six months after winning a modest lottery prize, equivalent to eight months' worth of income. It also found that the win had no effect on happiness.[2]

> Happiness is not a set of desirable life circumstances. It's a way of traveling.
>
> *Ed Diener*

You might be thinking that's just fine because you're not about to gamble your hard-earned cash, let alone play the ludicrous odds of a lottery. We're with you. But what about a pay raise? How would you feel about a little increase in your current income? Would twenty thousand dollars more put a big smile on your face? Of course. Research in psychology and economics has found that people *do* get happier as their income increases—but only up to a certain level.[3] Researchers find that life satisfaction rises with higher incomes up to a household income of about seventy-five thousand dollars. It levels off afterward.[4] In other words, money doesn't make us happy so much as it prevents us from being miserable. Still, that doesn't stop the vast majority of us from believing that more money, regardless of our income, would make us happier.

The First Half of Your Happiness— Your Set Point

As it turns out, people are not very good at predicting what will make them happy and how long that happiness will last. They expect positive events to make them much happier than those events actually do, and they expect negative events to make them unhappier than they actually do.[5] In both field and lab studies, we've found that passing or failing an exam, winning or losing an election, gaining or losing a great house, getting or not getting a promotion, and even getting married all have less impact on happiness than people think they will. A recent study showed that very few experiences affect us for more than three months. When good things happen, we celebrate for a while and then sober up. When bad things happen, we weep and whine for a while and then pick ourselves up and get on with it. Scientists call it *habituation*. The rest of us call it surprising. After all, you'd think that the thing we're pining for would make us happier than it actually does.

> It isn't what you have or who you are or where you are or what you are doing that makes you happy or unhappy. It is what you think about it.
>
> *Dale Carnegie*

It all has to do with what experts call our *happiness set point*. In fact, they say that 50 percent of our happiness is determined by our genes.[6] We have a range of happiness, we naturally fall into regardless of what happens. And generally speaking, we eventually return to our happiness set point even after a tremendous high or a deep low.

With a skull cap containing 128 sensors, Dr. Richard Davidson and his research team at the University of Wisconsin have been watching people's brains respond to happy as well as distressing circumstances. Their ongoing study aims to understanding how much of our joy level is set at birth, and how much we can control.

People with happy brains have their parents to thank, to a certain extent, not only for happy genes, according to Davidson, but also for loving childhoods. His studies as well as many others have shown that angry or critical parents can actually alter where a child's happiness level eventually rests until it's set around age sixteen.[7]

The bottom line? Half of our happiness is determined by a combination of our biological heredity and early upbringing. While our happiness will seesaw following pleasing or traumatic life events, it will inevitably shift back to a natural level.[8]

But this accounts for just 50 percent of our happiness factor. Which raises a question: What about the other half of our happiness? Can we stretch the limits of our preprogrammed temperaments to be happier?

The Second Half of Your Happiness— Your Choices

If our happiness set point is on the low end, making us less happy than others, are we doomed to stay that way? Hardly. The remaining portion of our happiness is within our control.

We take that back. Actually it's closer to 40 percent of the remaining portion of our happiness. Why? Because our circumstances account for about 10 percent of our happiness. In other words, having a job that pays enough money to meet our needs and being relatively healthy are circumstances that contribute to our overall happiness picture. But keep in mind this is only 10 percent. We underscore the percentage because most of us tend to bank so much of our happiness on our circumstances—just as the lottery winners do. We think that moving to a new house or a new city, securing a raise, or changing our appearance will make us happier. But we

> You don't find happiness, you make happiness.
>
> *David Leonhardt*

are unlikely to find lasting happiness by changing our life circumstances. Why? Because of our happiness set point and our inclination to adapt to positive circumstantial changes so quickly.

Thankfully, lasting happiness does not lie mainly in increasing our set point or positively impacting our circumstances. It's found in the remaining 40 percent of the happiness pie—and that's completely determined by us.[9] This significant portion of our happiness comes down to the choices we make, and they have nothing to do with our genetic make up or our circumstances. Happy people aren't just sitting around being happy. They are making happiness happen. And so are happy couples. They are pursuing happiness through intentional activities.

And what are these activities? Well, they're not difficult. They don't cost more money. And they don't consume inordinate amounts of time. The habits of happy couples are doable for any and all of us. To live at a level of happiness that surpasses our natural set point, enduring happiness only asks that we change a bit of how we think and behave. It's like weight. We all have a set point for weight, and if it's higher than we'd like we exercise and eat well daily to ensure we stay below that level. The same is true for happiness. We can boost our happiness above our preset level with a bit of effort. Ideally, that effort will become habit. Those prone to be less happy than others aren't doomed. They just have to try a smidge harder to counteract the forces working against them. In fact, research reveals that all of us can actually fix our happiness set point to be permanently higher.

> Whoever is happy will make others happy.
>
> *Anne Frank*

Sonja Lyubomirsky of the University of California, Riverside; Kennon M. Sheldon of the University of Missouri-Columbia; and

David A. Schkade of the University of California, San Diego, summarized numerous findings and put them into a simple pie chart showing what determines happiness:[10]

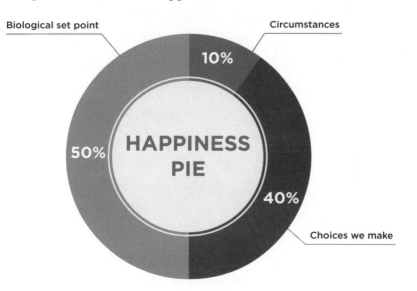

The Hat Trick of Happiness

This book is dedicated to helping the two of you form habits of happiness together. Not just any habits—the ones we know have a proven impact on your shared happiness. You've seen them in the table of contents of this book. They include counting your blessings, trying new things, adding value to others, and so on. We'll get to all of them shortly. But we first want you to know what they have in common and why they work to boost happiness that endures.

Pioneering researcher Martin Seligman outlined the ingredients for lasting happiness more than a decade ago: pleasure, engagement, and meaning.[11] We call them the hat trick of happiness. While they aren't weighted equally in what they can do for our happiness factor, they each add to our overall well-being and joy.

Pleasure

There's no denying the fact that pleasurable activity and experiences heighten our happiness. Consider ice cream. Not the kind that comes in a square block from the freezer section of your grocery store. We're talking about the kind that's handmade in small batches using only all-natural dairy. We're talking about the kind that's churned with very little air so that the flavor of caramel peanut clusters or mint chocolate chip dances on your tongue. The pleasure of this cold and creamy concoction can't help but make you happy.

> Remember this: very little is needed to make a happy life.
> *Marcus Aurelius*

Get the idea? Or how about a great movie that takes you on a thrill ride you didn't expect. A fantastic meal, relaxing conversation, great sex—all are gratifying pleasures. Pleasurable activities have a clear sensory and emotional component. They're all fun and they make us happy, especially when savored. In fact, the more we savor and relish our pleasures, the more happiness they bring. Not only that, but our pleasures are seemingly doubled when we experience them with the person we love. Sharing a pleasurable experience with the person you love is the single strongest predictor of improving pleasure. So as you'll soon see, many of our happiness boosters involve savoring pleasure together.

Engagement

Recently we sat on the floor in a crowded airline terminal and played a game of Scrabble on our trusty iPad. We had about thirty minutes to kill before we could board our flight and a quick game would do the trick. We've had a longstanding competition in our marriage with this game. We play to win. And on this occasion the game was especially tight. The score was teetering back and forth with nearly every move. Triple word scores hung in the balance. It was anyone's game.

It was also time to board our flight and we barely heard the announcement from the agent. We'd lost track of where we were and how much time had passed. We had to scramble to gather our belongings and get on the plane.

That's engagement. Researchers sometimes call it *flow* and it has to do with a state of being so wrapped up in an activity that we lose ourselves in it.

Does flow equal happiness? Not exactly. If you were to ask us what we felt in the midst of our Scrabble competition we would have likely said, "Nothing." We were just passing time. But it was the engagement of our minds and our beings in the process that brought about a sense of satisfaction that heightened happiness.

Of course engagement doesn't require competition. Engagement can ensue while tending a garden, talking together about your goals and dreams on a road trip, playing or listening to music, working on a home-improvement project, or preparing for an important milestone. Anything that includes the loss of self-consciousness during an absorbing activity is engagement. It's the process of merging with what we are doing because it consumes us.

Meaning

While delighting in hand-dipped ice cream is fun and becoming consumed in a game of Scrabble can engender contentment, this third ingredient of happiness trumps both pleasure and engagement. And happiness without meaning creates a relatively shallow, self-absorbed, or even selfish life.

Every dedicated parent knows the experience of sacrificing for a child. And every loving parent will tell you that the sacrifice is fulfilling. It seems implausible, but it's true. Paradoxically, a parent's happiness is raised by the very fact that they are willing to have their own happiness lowered through years of dirty diapers, tantrums, and backtalk. Willingness to accept unhappiness from children is a source of happiness. Why? In a word: meaning. Raising a child is one of the most meaningful endeavors we can take on.

Of course you don't have a to be a parent to experience meaning. We find meaning anytime we dedicate ourselves to something bigger than we are. Volunteering to help in a blood drive, sponsoring a needy child, mentoring a less experienced couple, or helping out in the life of your church all create meaning.

Consider an exercise we do every year with our university students in Seattle. In a class of 200 students, we assign half of them to take an afternoon and indulge themselves in something they think will make them happy. They might play video games, watch a movie, enjoy a great meal, and so on. We assign the other half of the students to take an afternoon and give themselves away by doing good for others. They might volunteer at a senior center, pick up litter around campus, help a student with special needs, and so on. When the next class meets we assess their happiness and guess what we find? You got it. The group that does good for others is inevitably and consistently much happier than the group that indulged themselves in something that gave them pleasure. It's tough to trump love and meaning when it comes to happiness.

> Love is the condition in which the happiness of another person is essential to your own.
>
> *Robert Heinlein*

Get this: people who have meaning in their lives, in the form of a defined purpose, rate their satisfaction with life higher even when they feel worse than those who do not have a clearly defined purpose. Is it any wonder that *The Purpose Driven Life* by Rick Warren is the bestselling hardcover book in American history?[12] Meaning and purpose are essential to abiding happiness.

Pleasure, engagement, and meaning—the hat trick of happiness. Each of these ingredients is essential to leveraging the remaining 40 percent of the happiness within our control. They are the three big dials we can turn to counter our circumstances and genes. But beware: pursuing pleasure by itself brings only temporary happiness. Pleasure alone has no lasting impact. Think of watching a fun TV show, or if you're a shopper, going to the mall. It's enjoyable in the moment. Then the fun is over. Yet far too many people believe pleasure is the only road to happiness. It's not. In fact, it's the least enduring and fulfilling. Engagement provides a deeper satisfaction that typically persists after the activity is finished. And meaning provides the greatest and most enduring satisfaction of all. Together, pleasure, engagement, and meaning make for a full life.[13]

> The greatest happiness in the world is the conviction that we are loved; loved for ourselves, or rather, loved in spite of ourselves.
>
> *Victor Hugo*

The Happiest Place on Earth?

The Danes must be doing something right. Denmark recently ranked as the happiest nation on the planet, according to the World Map of Happiness.[14] The happiest city on the globe, however, is half a world away in Singapore. Ninety-five percent of its citizens say they are either very happy or quite happy.[15] You'll find the United States among the twenties when its happiness is ranked. And the happiest US city? Boulder, Colorado, is often at or near the top spot according to the National Well-Being Index.[16] Who knew?

Money can't buy happiness. But it sure can buy the ability to measure it. Several organizations and governments spend millions on expert teams of researchers and statisticians who measure happiness across the world. But nobody takes happiness more seriously than a little country in South Asia. While most countries like America are busy measuring their Gross Domestic Product (the market value of all our good and services we produce), the Himalayan country of Bhutan is actually more concerned with raising its Gross National Happiness.

> It's pretty hard to tell what does bring happiness. Poverty and wealth have both failed.
>
> *Ken Hubbard*

It all makes sense, if you think about it. As the old adage in business says, what gets measured gets managed. And the better we measure happiness, the better we cultivate it—whether it's on a global or personal level. That's why we want to help take inventory of your own happy factor. And it's easier than you think.

Measuring Your Personal Happy Factor

They call him the Indiana Jones of happiness research. For almost forty years, Dr. Ed Diener has been a professor of psychology at the University of Illinois. But his quest to accurately measure people's happiness has taken him to exotic populations ranging from the Maasai in Africa to the Inuit in Greenland. And his happiness inventory below is among the most widely used and respected instruments around.[17] It will take you just a couple of minutes.

Your Happy Factor Assessment

Use the scale of 1 to 7 below to rate your agreement or disagreement with the following five statements. Simply place the appropriate number on the line preceding it. Please be open and honest in your responding.

7–Strongly agree   3–Slightly disagree
6–Agree   2–Disagree
5–Slightly agree   1–Strongly disagree
4–Neither agree
    nor disagree

_____ In most ways my life is close to my ideal.

_____ The conditions of my life are excellent.

_____ I am satisfied with my life.

_____ So far I have gotten the important things I want in life.

_____ If I could live my life over, I would change almost nothing.

_____ TOTAL Score

What Your Score Means

31–35 Extremely Satisfied: You love your life and feel things are going very well. Of course, just because you are so fulfilled does not mean you're complacent. You likely realize that your well-being is always in a process that requires tending to continue to grow. That's why you're invested in this book and you are sure to get a great deal of its message because of that.

26–30 Satisfied: You like your life and feel that things are going well. Life is enjoyable, but you also realize that you can maximize your life and live it more fully. In all likelihood, you like the idea of striving to bring more fulfillment into your life and that will bode well for you as your explore this book.

21–25 Slightly Satisfied: The majority of people in economically developed nations score here. While you're generally satisfied, you would very much like some improvement. You are probably ready for some changes that will boost your happiness. And that's exactly what you'll find in this book.

15–20 Slightly Dissatisfied: You probably have a few small but significant issues in various areas of your life, or you may have just one area that's a substantial challenge. Regardless, some changes are in order and this book will help you zero your efforts in on activities that will give you the greatest payoff.

10–14 Dissatisfied: You're not doing so well. It may be one big issue or several that are going badly. If your dissatisfaction is in response to a recent event such as bereavement, you will likely return over time to your former level of higher satisfaction. Of course, if your dissatisfaction in life has been chronically low, we urge you to see a trusted counselor or pastor.

5–9 Extremely Dissatisfied: You're obviously very unhappy with your current life. You may have experienced a recent bad event such as unemployment or you may have a chronic problem such as an addiction or alcoholism. However, dissatisfaction at this level is typically due to multiple problem areas. Whatever the reason, we urge you to see a competent psychologist, counselor, or minister. This is not a journey to travel alone.

So Happy Together

As we wrap up this chapter and launch into the heart of this book, the happiness boosters, we want to make it abundantly clear: your happiness does not depend on your partner. It's not his or her job to make you happy. Happiness is an *inside* job. We said it earlier and we want to underscore it again. Marriage doesn't make you happy. You make your marriage happy. A common mistake is to say, "I used to be happy, then I got married, and now I'm not as happy as I used to be," and conclude there's something wrong with the marriage. Nope. You're just not turning the right dials to increase the happy factor in your marriage. You need to make happy together. And the next part of this book is dedicated to helping you and your partner do exactly that.

But, you may be asking, *can I do these happiness boosters if my partner doesn't want to join in? Will it still pay off and increase my well-being in the relationship?* Absolutely. Why? Because happiness begins on the inside and is very contagious.

A Dutch scientist, Christiaan Huygens, back in the 1660s realized that two pendulums mounted on the same wall always ended up swinging in perfect synchrony, even when they had been set in motion at different times. The phenomenon is call *entrainment*, and it happens with husbands and wives as well. When one person begins to take on a new attitude or behavior in the relationship, the other often falls in sync. Research backs this idea up.[18]

So if you begin practicing some of these boosters on your own, your partner is likely to eventually join in. As Ed Diener says, "Happiness is not a set of desirable life circumstances. It's a way of traveling." And we're confident you're going to enjoy this journey.

For Reflection

1. Would making more money make you happier? If so, how much more money and why or how would it elevate your mood over the long run?

2. What do you make of the fact that 40 percent of your happiness is determined by your choices? Do you agree? Why or why not? And what choices have you made this week that have led to long-term happiness with your partner?

3. How do you feel about the results of your happy factor self test? Do you agree with them? Why or why not? What about your partner's results?

PART TWO

Happiness Boosters for Couples

3 Count Your Blessings

> It is not happiness that makes us grateful, but
> gratefulness that makes us happy.
>
> *Brother David Steindl-Rast*

WE'D JUST FLOWN INTO Phoenix, Arizona, late at night, checked into a hotel, and turned on the television to hear this: "Everything's amazing right now, but nobody's happy." It was the first line in a routine by comedian Louis C. K., who was chatting it up on Conan O'Brien's talk show. "In my lifetime the changes in the world have been incredible," he said. He went on to describe how we used to have rotary phones that you'd dial and stand next to. "And then if you called and they weren't home, the phone would just ring lonely by itself."

Today we carry phones in our pockets, untethered by wires, and people complain that it won't work fast enough. "Give it a second! It's going to space," said C. K. "Will you give it a second to get back from space? Is the speed of light too slow for you?"

He talked about how he was on a plane that offered in-flight Wi-Fi access to the Internet—one of the first planes to do so. But when it broke down in a few minutes, the man sitting next to him swore in disgust. C. K. was amazed and said to O'Brien, "How quickly the world owes him something that he didn't know existed ten seconds ago."

C. K. then talked about how many of us describe less-than-perfect airline flights as if they were experiences from a horror film:

Praise the bridge that carried you over.

George Colman

"It was the worst day of my life. First of all, we didn't board for twenty minutes! And then we get on the plane and they made us sit there on the runway for forty minutes!"

Then he said mockingly, "Oh, really? Did you fly through the air incredibly, like a bird? Did you partake in the miracle of human flight ... Everybody on every plane should be screaming, 'Wow!' You're sitting in a chair in the sky!" And then he mocked a passenger who, trying to push his seat back, complained, "It doesn't go back a lot!"[1]

It's funny because it's true. Right? In fact, it was a little too true for us. We'd just experienced one of those less-than-perfect flying days and we'd been pretty free with our complaints throughout the ordeal. And not once did we pause to acknowledge how privileged we were to be giving a marriage seminar the next morning or how great it was that we were traveling together, that we loved each other, that we were getting to watch a movie on the flight from Seattle and getting to have dinner the next evening with good friends while we were in town. Nope. We focused on the airline delay, the lack of food options, and the seats that didn't go back a lot. Gratitude didn't even enter the picture.

Chances are you know exactly what we're talking about. We've all been there—complaining about something when we have so much to be grateful for. It's an attitude of discontent that breeds entitlement. It can permeate our lives if we're not careful. Actually, it permeates our lives—including our marriage—if we're not grateful.

Defining Gratitude

Some say gratitude is what gets poured into the glass to make it half full. Perhaps. A thankful heart *does* engender optimism. But the dictionary is more specific: "the quality or feeling of being thankful." No surprise there. Yet when you scratch beneath the surface and explore its Latin root, *gratia*, you'll find that gratitude is related to the words *grace* and *gift*. Gratitude results from unmerited favor, separate from our own striving, and requires no payment or debt.

Gratitude is not the same as indebtedness.[2] While they are similar, indebtedness occurs when a person perceives that they are under an obligation to make repayment to the person who has helped them. Indebtedness can cause you to avoid the person who has helped you out. Gratitude, on the other hand, like a grace gift, motivates you to seek out the person and improve the relationship. It implies humility—an acknowledgment that we could not be who we are or where we are without the kind gifts we receive from others.

> Gratitude is an opener of locked-up blessings.
> *Marianne Williamson*

A spirit of gratitude acknowledges that others, including our spouse, friends, and God, gave us many gifts, big and small, to help us achieve the goodness in our lives. Gratitude is a relationship-strengthening spirit. It's more than a feeling. It's an attitude, a habit, a choice, a motive, a way of life.[3] Perhaps that's why Cicero, the Roman philosopher, said, "Gratitude is not only the greatest of virtues, but the parent of all the others."

What's Your Gratitude Quotient?

How well do you express appreciation to your spouse? How grateful do you feel in general? This little assessment may shed some light for you on your personal gratitude quotient. Use the scale below as a guide to note a number beside each statement to indicate how much you agree with it.[4]

7–Strongly agree   3–Slightly disagree
6–Agree   2–Disagree
5–Slightly agree   1–Strongly disagree
4–Neither agree
    nor disagree

_____ 1. I have so much in life to be thankful for.

_____ 2. If I had to list everything that I felt grateful for, it would be a very long list.

_____ 3. When I look at the world, I don't see much to be grateful for.

_____ 4. I am grateful to a wide variety of people.

_____ 5. As I get older, I find myself more able to appreciate the people, events, and situations that have been part of my life history.

_____ 6. Long amounts of time can go by before I feel grateful to something or someone.

Scoring

Add up your scores for items 1, 2, 4, and 5. Write the subtotal here: _____

Reverse your scores for items 3 and 6. That is, if you scored a 7, give yourself a 1, if you scored a 6, give yourself a 2, etc. Write the subtotal here: _____

Add the subtotals from Steps 1 and 2. This is your total GQ-6 score. This number should be between 6 and 42. Write it here: _____

Benchmarks

Curious to know where you stand on your gratitude quotient compared to other people (including your partner)? If you scored 35 or below, then you are in the bottom one-fourth of people who have taken this survey, meaning 75 percent of people feel more gratitude than you do. If you scored between 36 and 38, you are in the bottom one-half of people who took the survey. If you scored between 39 and 41, you are in the top one-fourth, and if you scored 42, you are in the top one-eighth.

Of course, this self-report survey is only as good as you are in being honest about your answers and it's simply meant to serve as a means for you to better reflect on your relationship with gratitude. Regardless of your score, or that of your partner's, everyone can benefit from learning to be more grateful.

How More Gratitude
Boosts Your Happiness

"The doors of happiness remain locked," said Fawn Weaver, founder of the Happy Wives Club Web site. "When they are unlocked, they swing open quickly and widely but close right behind them. They must be reopened throughout each day and there is but one key that fits that lock: Gratitude."

Studies back up this poetic notion. A growing body of research has tied an attitude of gratitude to numerous benefits, including happiness and more. The *Wall Street Journal* summarized the research: adults who frequently feel grateful have more energy, more optimism, more social connections, and more happiness than those who do not. They're also less likely to be depressed, envious, or greedy. They earn more money, sleep more soundly, exercise more regularly, and have greater resistance to illness.[5] Not a bad bundle of benefits.

> Gratitude can transform common days into thanksgivings, turn routine jobs into joy, and change ordinary opportunities into blessings.
>
> *William Arthur Ward*

But there's an even more astounding and measurable benefit to our well-being when it comes to cultivating gratitude. After research involving thousands of people, conducted by a number of different researchers around the world, Dr. Robert Emmons—who has been studying gratitude for more than a decade and is considered by many to be the world's leading authority on the subject—said this: studies show that practicing gratitude can increase happiness levels by around 25 percent.

Not bad, right? How would your life and your relationship look if over the next few days if you became 25 percent happier? How would your relationship look if your partner were suddenly 25 percent happier? It's impossible to separate gratitude from happiness. You can't have one without the other. And it's impossible to exaggerate what gratitude can do to boost the level of happiness in your marriage.

What Gratitude Does for Your Relationship

A man accompanied his friend home for dinner and was impressed by the way he entered his house, asked his wife how her day went, and told her she looked pretty. Then, after they embraced, she served dinner. After they ate, the husband complimented his wife on the meal and thanked her for it. When the two fellows were alone, the visitor asked, "Why do you treat your wife so well?"

"Because she deserves it, and it makes our marriage happier," replied the host.

Impressed, the visitor decided to adopt the idea. Arriving home, he embraced his wife and said, "You look wonderful!" For good measure he added, "Sweetheart, I'm the luckiest guy in the world."

> Let us be grateful to the people who make us happy; they are the charming gardeners who make our souls blossom.
>
> *Marcel Proust*

His wife burst into tears. Bewildered, he asked her, "What in the world's the matter?"

She wept. "What a day! Billy fought at school. The refrigerator quit and spoiled the groceries. And now you've come home drunk!"

It's an old joke but it underscores a vital point: gratitude in marriage can become so rare that when it appears we may think there's something wrong. As marriages move past the honeymoon stage, couples go from appreciating and loving every little detail about each other to taking each other wholly for granted. The antidote? Without question, it's gratitude.

Gratitude is literally one of the few things that can instantly and measurably improve a couple's relationship. The benefits of gratitude in a relationship are calculable.

A study asked couples to report nightly for two weeks how grateful they felt toward their partners from their day's interactions. In addition to gratitude, they numerically rated their relationship satisfaction and their feelings of connection with their partner. What did they find? On days that people felt more gratitude toward their partner, they felt better about their relationship and more connected to their partner. Not only that, they also experienced greater happiness and satisfaction in their relationship the *following* day.[6] In other words, gratitude helps happiness linger.

But the benefits didn't stop there. The partners of these grateful people felt more connected and were happier and more satisfied with the relationship too—and they weren't the one's recording their gratitude. Amazing! Happiness that stems from gratitude is contagious in a relationship.

Another experiment, this time with dating couples, had people list nice things their partners had done for them lately and rate how well they thought they had expressed appreciation to their partner for having done those favors. The researchers found that the more they expressed appreciation the more they decreased the odds of breaking up.

The bottom line is this: moments of gratitude act as a booster shot for romantic relationships. Gratitude elevates, energizes, and inspires more love.

How to Count Your Blessings Together

Ready to infuse your relationship with more gratitude? Well, here's what works. Each of these tips is based on research and has proven effective for countless couples. Because everyone is different, however, you'll likely find that some are more helpful to you than others.

Make Gratitude Your Thing

One of the most revealing experiments to ever connect gratitude and happiness was conducted by Robert Emmons, a professor of psychology at the University of California, Davis and psychology professor Michael McCullough of Southern Methodist University in Dallas, Texas. They took three groups of volunteers and randomly assigned them to focus on one of three things each week: hassles, things for which they were grateful, and ordinary life events.[7]

The first group concentrated on everything that went wrong or that irritated them. The second group honed in on situations they felt enhanced their lives, such as, "My husband is so kind and caring—I'm lucky to have him." The third group recalled recent everyday events such as, "I went shoe shopping."

> You have to participate relentlessly in the manifestation of your own blessings.
>
> *Elizabeth Gilbert*

The results: the people who focused on gratitude were happier by far. They saw their lives in favorable terms. They reported positive feelings and fewer negative complaints, and they even reported experiencing better health (fewer headaches and colds). They also offered more grace to others and did more loving things for people. Those who were grateful quite simply enjoyed a higher quality of life.

Dr. Emmons was surprised. He found that this is not just something that makes people happy, like positive thinking. A feeling of gratitude really gets people to do something, to become more compassionate, more loving. Such was not the case in either of the other two groups.

> Feeling gratitude and not expressing it is like wrapping a present and not giving it.
>
> *William Arthur Ward*

The point is obvious: your life is never more filled with joy than when you are conscious of your blessings. People who feel grateful are more likely to feel loved as well as do loving things. And all it takes is a conscious effort to be mindful of your blessings. Gratitude is a discipline. You can choose to be grateful. You can make it your thing.

The late Catholic priest, psychologist, and writer Henri Nouwen said it this way: "It is amazing how many occasions present themselves in which I can choose gratitude instead of complaint." So true. Every day we have moments where we sidestep a conscious effort to be grateful because we feel entitled or we've taken something for granted. But once we decide to be more grateful, gratitude appears. So the first step in bringing more gratitude into your life and your relationship is merely choosing to be thankful. It's as simple as that.

Curb Complaints

An efficiency expert concluded a lecture with a note of caution: "You don't want to try these techniques at home."

"Why not?" asked someone from the back of the audience.

"I watched my wife's routine at breakfast for years," the expert explained. "She made lots of trips to the refrigerator, stove, table, and cabinets, often carrying just a single item at a time. 'Honey,' I suggested, 'Why don't you try carrying several things at once?'"

The person in the audience asked, "Did it save time?"

The expert replied, "Actually, yes. It used to take her twenty minutes to get breakfast ready. Now I do it in seven."

Nothing extinguishes gratitude more quickly than complaining—especially in marriage. And yet it's so easy to fall into the trap of grumbling. The average person complains between twenty and thirty times per day. We grouse and moan almost out of habit.

So how can you curb complaints? Will Bowman, a Kansas City minister, has the answer. He challenged his congregation to go twenty-one days without complaining. He based his challenge on research suggesting that it takes at least twenty-one days to form a new habit. People who took the challenge were issued a little purple wristband as a reminder of their pledge. If they caught themselves complaining, they were supposed to take off the bracelet, switch it to the opposite wrist, and start counting the days from scratch.

> Entitlement turns us into complainers.
>
> *Tullian Tchividjian*

Rev. Bowen said it took him three and a half months to put together twenty-one complaint-free days, and that it has taken others up to seven months. Those who get through it can turn in their bracelets in exchange for Certificates of Happiness issued during church services.[8]

Whether you are ready to take the twenty-one-day challenge with a purple wristband or not, we suggest trying something that may require a little more courage—if only for a week. It's not easy, but it's the best way we've found to curb complaining in our own relationship. Ready? You simply make a pact to help each other stifle grumbles by inviting nonthreatening feedback. For us, that means we agree form the letter *C* with our hand and show it to each other whenever we notice the other person complaining. And when we see our partner giving this signal we simply respond with "Thank you." That's it. We don't condemn or correct. We simply flash a momentary sign that we've both asked each other to provide for us. Try it for seven days and we guarantee you'll see your complaining diminish while your gratitude rises.

Keep a Gratitude Journal

Did you know that people who write their goals down, as opposed to just thinking about them, are 33 percent more likely to accomplish them? There's something powerful about writing things down. And this applies to gratitude as well.

At the University of California at Riverside, psychologist Sonja Lyubomirsky is using grant money from the National Institutes of Health to study different kinds of happiness boosters. And writing in a gratitude journal—a diary in which you write down things for which you are thankful—is proving to be one of the most effective. She has found that taking the time to conscientiously count your blessings once a week significantly increases your overall satisfaction with life over a period of six weeks (compared to a control group that did not keep journals and had no such gain).

> There is not a more pleasing exercise of the mind than gratitude.
>
> *Joseph Addison*

In addition to heightening their overall happiness level, those who kept a gratitude journal experienced longer-lasting positive effects. Their happiness continued to increase each time they were tested periodically after the experiment. In fact, the greatest benefits were usually found to occur around six months after the process began. The exercise was so successful that although participants were only asked to continue the journal for a week, many participants continued to keep the journal long after the study was over.[9]

If the idea of starting a gratitude journal strikes your fancy, here are a few tips to keep in mind:

- *Don't just go through the motions.* Research by Lyubomirsky and others suggests that journaling is more effective if you first make the conscious decision to become more grateful. The act of keeping the journal does nothing if you're heart isn't in it.
- *Go for depth over breadth.* Elaborating in detail about a particular thing for which you're grateful carries more benefits than a superficial list of many things.
- *Get personal.* Focusing on *people* to whom you are grateful has more of an impact than focusing on *things* for which you are grateful. This is particularly true when you focus on your spouse.
- *Try subtraction, not just addition.* One effective way of stimulating gratitude is to reflect on what your life would be like *without* certain blessings, rather than just tallying up all those good things.
- *Savor surprises.* Try to record events that were unexpected or surprising, as these tend to elicit stronger levels of gratitude. For example, a surprise visit for lunch from your spouse.

- *Don't overdo it.* Writing occasionally (once per week) is more beneficial than daily journaling. In fact, one study by Lyubomirsky and her colleagues found that people who wrote in their gratitude journals once a week reported boosts in happiness afterward; people who wrote three times per week didn't.[10]

Ready to give it a try? Simply write down three things you're grateful for once a week—and share them with your spouse. And if you'd like to put a new spin on it, try a shared gratitude journal. It's easy. If you both agree, one of you starts by making your entries into the journal and then places it somewhere for your partner to do the same. You simply pass it back and forth every so often, allowing each of you to read each other's entries and be inspired by what you're both writing. No need to set strict timelines on when you do it. Make it casual. And of course bring it up in your conversations when you're ready. You're sure to note a measurable increase in your shared happiness when you keep a gratitude journal.

Plan a Gratitude Visit

This is likely the most challenging suggestion in this chapter—but also the most rewarding. It began in a classroom at the University of Pennsylvania when Martin Seligman had his students select an important person in their pasts who had "made a major positive difference in your life and to whom you have never fully expressed your thanks."[11]

Next, Dr. Seligman had them take their time to write a one-page testimonial expressing what that person had done for them and how grateful they were for the good they brought into their life. Then he had his students arrange an in-person meeting with the individual (not on the phone or in writing), without telling them the purpose for the meeting. They were then directed to read the testimonial aloud slowly, with expression, and with eye contact, allowing the other person to react unhurriedly.

Since the time of this first classroom assignment in 2004, Seligman has conducted controlled experiments on the effects of this exercise and witnessed its power through reports from thousands of gratitude visits. The single most effective way to turbocharge your joy, he says, is to make a gratitude visit.

Are you game? Are you willing to write a thoughtful testimonial thanking a teacher, pastor, or grandparent—anyone to whom you are deeply grateful—and then visit that person to read him or her the letter of appreciation? If you do, you're sure to feel a surge in joy wash over you and see the same in the person you're appreciating.

And if you're willing to take this to a new level as a couple, we recommend a gratitude visit together. We did this some time ago with a couple who was particularly helpful to our marriage, Dennis and Lucy Guernsey. They'd been married longer than us by a decade or more and we looked to them as our marriage mentors. One evening in their home we read our letter of appreciation aloud to them. Part of the letter focused on how authentic and transparent they'd been with us. It was a true gift. We recounted the story they told us of the night, early in their marriage, when Lucy threw her wedding band in anger and

> The deepest craving of human nature is the need to be appreciated.
>
> *William James*

how they later found reconciliation and forgiveness. It didn't take long before we were all in tears. They were tears of joy, of course, and the joy lasts to this day. This gratitude visit together became all the more poignant and meaningful when we learned Dennis was diagnosed with a brain tumor. He passed away at age fifty-eight less than a year later.

Savor Good Moments

Coca-Cola was invented in 1886 by a pharmacist named "Doc" John Pemberton. He fought in the Civil War, and at the end of the war, living in Atlanta, he saw that soda fountains were rising in popularity. By 1920 Coca-Cola could be found in 99 percent of the soda fountains across the United States.

While Pemberton invented it, a man named Asa Candler sold it. Candler firmly believed in the importance of advertising, which led him to distribute thousands of complimentary tickets for free glasses of Coca-Cola. He also believed in promoting the beverage on outdoor posters, calendars, soda fountain urns, and even wall murals (this was before billboards). He also came up with one of the most successful marketing slogans ever: "The Pause That Refreshes."

> Remember that what you now have was once among the things you only hoped for.
>
> *Epicurus*

The slogan made its debut in the *Saturday Evening Post* just before the onset of the Great Depression. It made the point that men and women work better if given a few breaks in their workday. Coca-Cola's per capita consumption doubled that year.

"The Pause that Refreshes" campaign lasted well into the 1950s. And the sentiment lives on to this day. After all, who doesn't want a refreshing moment to savor—even if it's just a cold, crisp soda?

Candler was tapping into a human experience long before it was ever studied.

To this day you'll find plenty of books on coping with life's negative events but what about enjoying the good events for all they're worth? That's the business of savoring.

"It's been presumed that when good things happen, people naturally feel joy for it," said Fred Bryant, a social psychologist at Loyola University Chicago. His research, however, suggests that we don't always respond to these "good things" in ways that maximize their positive effects on our lives.

Bryant is the father of research on *savoring*, or the concept that being mindfully engaged and aware of your feelings during positive events can increase happiness in the short and long run. What does he recommend for savoring the moment? Here you go:

- *Share your good feelings with others—especially your spouse.* "Savoring is the glue that bonds people together, and it is essential to prolonging relationships," Bryant said. "People who savor together stay together."
- *Take a mental picture.* Consciously be aware of things you want to remember later, such as the sound of your partner's laugh or a touching moment between two family members. Seize it in your mind.
- *Sharpen your senses.* Taking the time to use your senses more consciously flexes your savoring muscles. You can do this by shutting out other senses to hone in on one. For example, studies reveal that if people enjoy the aroma of a nice dish of pasta before they eat it, they'll enjoy the taste even more. This means slowing down while you eat—a key to savoring.

- *Absorb the moment.* Try to turn off your desire to multitask and instead remain in the here and now. If you're taking in a work of art, tuning in to a message on your phone removes you from the pleasure.

- *Enjoy the passage of time.* Good moments pass quickly, so you've got to consciously relish them. Realizing how short lived certain moments are and wishing they could last longer encourages you to enjoy them while they're happening. You can simply tell yourself, "This is such a good day, and I know I'll look back with good memories."

The point of savoring is to make positive experiences last by staying with them rather than allowing your attention to skitter off to something else while the positive moment quickly fades.

A Final Thought on Counting Your Blessings Together

> If you concentrate on finding whatever is good in every situation, you will discover that your life will suddenly be filled with gratitude, a feeling that nurtures the soul.
>
> *Harold Kushner*

Gratitude is a power booster to being happy in love. No doubt about it. But if you're struggling a bit to turn the dial up on gratitude in your relationship, we want to leave you with a proven motivator to get you started. It has to do with imagining life without your partner. It's a jolt to the heart, but it may be the jolt that sparks appreciation that's lain dormant too long.

In *Lisey's Story*, prolific author Stephen King told the fictional story of a widow two years after her husband's death. "I lay awake and listened to the clock on your nightstand and the wind outside and understood that I was really home," said Lisey, "that in bed with you was home . . . My heart cracked with gratitude. I think it was the first gratitude I've ever really known. I lay there beside you and the tears rolled down the sides of my face and onto the pillow. I loved you then and I love you now and I have loved you every second in between."[12]

You don't need a tragedy to have your heart crack with gratitude. Just imagine what your life would be like without the person you love most. If you've taken each other for granted a little more than you'd like, it's time to rekindle gratitude for the gift you are to each other. And if your relationship has been bruised upon the rocky shore, it's all the more important to know that struggles end when gratitude begins.

For Reflection

1. What do you make of your score on the self-assessment of gratitude in this chapter? What does it tell you? How does it compare with your partner's? Take a moment to discuss your scores together.
2. What do you make of starting a gratitude journal? Is this something you would like to do? Why or why not? What is most likely to keep you from doing it?
3. As you ponder a gratitude visit, is there a couple that comes to mind who has mentored you in your relationship and to whom you'd like to express your appreciation? If not, what individuals would be on your top two or three list of potential recipients? How likely are you to do this exercise?

4 Try New Things

Children are happy because they don't have a file in their minds called "All the Things That Could Go Wrong."

Marianne Williamson

"YOU SIGNED US UP for what?"

"A trapeze class," Les said.

"As in 'flew through the air with the greatest of ease' kind of trapeze?"

"Yes. I found a special they were running with Groupon—it's like half price or something." Les was speaking as if he'd ordered us a couple of ham sandwiches.

"I'm not concerned about the money. I'm concerned about our safety."

"They start us off in 'Ground School' before we do tricks in the air and stuff," he said with a straight face. "It will be fun."

"Have you lost your mind?" I blurted out. "I have no desire to join Ringling Brothers."

Les laughed out loud at my apprehension and began showing me photos on the Web site. The pictures did little to ease my anxiety—but I eventually agreed to go along (just like Les knew I would).

When we entered the Aerialdrome, Les said, "See, they have a net under the whole thing so you can't get hurt if you fall." I was looking at the trapeze platform that was at least twenty-five feet in the air when our instructor approached.

> We are plain quiet folk and have no use for adventures. Nasty disturbing uncomfortable things! Make you late for dinner!
>
> *J. R. R. Tolkien*

"You'll want to change your clothes and start warming up your muscles," the instructor told us. "It makes it much easier to hang from the bar by your knees."

I looked at Les, wide eyed, as we walked to our respective locker rooms. Les just grinned and bounced his eyebrows at me.

As it turned out, it wasn't nearly as bad as I thought it would be. After being hooked up to the rig around my waist and learning the takeoff techniques, I was in the air and learning to knee hang—thirty minutes into the lesson. Wow! And before the class was finished, after I got my courage up, I was flying into the hands of another instructor who caught me from the other trapeze. Wow again!

Sure, I was attached to a harness that keeps me from falling, and yes, there was a humongous bouncy net running the length of the set up, but this was not your average "dinner and a movie" date night. This was something out of the ordinary. This was an adventure.

And that's exactly what this chapter is dedicated to helping you do—experience more adventures. Don't worry, a high-flying trapeze act is not required. All we ask is that you explore how trying novel activities can impact your relationship. It's a secret the happiest couples know: experiencing new things together breeds deeper happiness and greater love.

Defining *Adventure*

"Adventure must start with running away from home," said British journalist William Bolitho. An adventure begins when we move out of our comfort zone. Familiarity precludes excitement. By definition, *adventure* is a thrilling or unusual experience. It's novel and new.

You sometimes hear people speak of the "spirit of adventure." They mean being a little daring and bold. They mean taking action. After all, as the saying goes, you can't cross the sea by merely standing and staring at the water. Adventure requires that you jump into the experience.

> To venture causes anxiety, but not to venture is to lose one's self.
>
> *Søren Kierkegaard*

Adventures, the Latin root, literally means "to arrive." When you're on an adventure you've already arrived at your destination, for it is the excitement of the journey that you're looking for, not an end place.

How Trying New Things Boosts Your Happiness

To figure out what people do in a typical day, interviewers talked to four thousand Americans. Study participants were asked to split up the prior day into fifteen-minute periods and relive what they did, who they were with, and how they felt. These four thousand people were selected to represent every part of the United States, matching census data on age, gender, ethnicity, and so on.

The findings? In a typical day we spend just over 17 percent of our time in activities that we find as enjoyable and meaningful. That's just twenty-five minutes per day doing what we love: sharing quality time with our spouse, listening to music, being in nature, and so on. And the vast majority of us spend nearly 20 percent of every day in unsatisfying activities such as commuting to work or fixing a broken appliance. The rest of our time is spent in the middle, passively accepting whatever the day holds.[1] Clearly the vast majority of us are not waking up and hollering "*Carpe diem!*" in the morning. We're not living with passion and an adventurous spirit.

> Don't be afraid to expand yourself, to step out of your comfort zone. That's where the joy and adventure lie.
>
> *Herbie Hancock*

Why is that? To be blunt, we play it safe. Life is going along okay. We're making it. We've found an easy groove in life and love. The only problem is that this groove, if we're not mindful, can eventually become a rut. And the longer we stay stuck in it, the less passion and happiness we experience.

A public opinion poll taken by the National Opinion Research Center found that over half of all adults in their twenties rate their lives as "exciting." Once people reach their forties this slips to 46 percent. At sixty it falls to 34 percent. The Noble Prize-winning French philosopher, physician, and musician Albert Schweitzer fervently believed, "The tragedy of life is what dies inside a person while they live."

Did you know that dopamine in the brain is essential to happiness? Maybe that's what Dr. Schweitzer was getting at. As we age we lose dopamine and it doesn't regenerate. In other words, we use it or lose it. The brain is like a muscle that needs novel exercise to keep it fit.

Trying new things does just that. It heightens our happiness. Psychologist Rich Walker of Winston-Salem State University and his team of researchers reviewed thirty thousand event memories recorded in over five hundred diaries, ranging from durations of three months to four years. What did they find? People who engage in a variety of novel experiences are more likely to experience and retain positive emotions and minimize negative ones. People who recorded fewer novel experiences experienced significantly less happiness and far more depression.[2]

Walker's advice? "Stop putting off seeing the aurora lights, warming up in the hot springs of Greenland or learning a new instrument—just do it. If you often do one thing that makes you happy, then try another."[3]

What's Your Adventure Quotient?

Are you an adventurous soul or are you inclined to huddle up in your comfort zone and play it safe. Take this little questionnaire to shed some light. Simply answer each question with honesty.

1. I get excited by the prospect of a new experience.

    Not at all   *Absolutely*
    1   2   3   4   5   6   7   8   9   10

2. Most people that know me would say I'm an adventurous spirit.

    Not at all   *Absolutely*
    1   2   3   4   5   6   7   8   9   10

3. I'm not afraid to do something that might be a little embar-
rassing if it means having a fun time.

Not at all   *Absolutely*
1   2   3   4   5   6   7   8   9   10

4. I'd rather try and fail than not try at all.

Not at all   *Absolutely*
1   2   3   4   5   6   7   8   9   10

5. I identify with this sentiment: being caught in the rain
by myself is a hassle, but being caught in the rain with
my partner is an adventure.

Not at all   *Absolutely*
1   2   3   4   5   6   7   8   9   10

Total Score: _____

Making Sense of Your Score

Your score can range anywhere between 5 and 50. The higher
your score, the more likely you are to be adventurous. In
other words, the easier it will be for you to try new things
together with your partner. Regardless of your score, however, everyone can push beyond their comfort zone and step
into an adventure. It's simply a matter of how hard you have
to work at it.

What Trying New Things Does for Your Relationship

The start of any romantic relationship is exciting, in part, because of the novelty of experiencing life with a new person. But research reveals that novelty wears thin starting at about two years into marriage. Fast-forward a decade or more and you'll likely find a couple whose life has become relatively routine—the same meals, the same TV shows, the same restaurants, the same vacation destinations, and the same conversations. And while familiarity can be comforting, it can also induce boredom. Routine rarely makes hearts race the way they once did.

Arthur Aron from the State University of New York at Stony Brook and his colleagues from various other universities were curious to see if they could help seasoned, married couples re-experience the thrill of dating and their early years together.[4] Specifically, would getting couples to break the monotony of married life rekindle romance and boost their happy factor?

Aron placed newspaper ads for couples who were willing to participate in an experiment exploring the "factors that affect relationships." When volunteers arrived at the lab, each couple completed a questionnaire about their relationship and was randomly assigned to one of two groups. The experimenters then cleared away the tables and chairs, rolled out some gym mats, and started the next part of the study.

> Being soaked alone is cold. Being soaked with your best friend is an adventure.
>
> *Emily Wing*

For half the couples, the researchers produced a roll of Velcro tape and explained that they were about to take part in a game. If the couples' eyes lit up and they exchanged knowing glances, the researchers quickly put the Velcro tape away and asked them to leave. For everyone else, the team used the Velcro to secure one person's right wrist to the left wrist of their partner, and also to strap their right and left ankles together.

The researchers placed a three-foot high foam obstacle in the middle of the room and handed each couple a large pillow. Each couple had to get on hands and knees, crawl up to the obstacle, climb over it, crawl to the other side of the room, turn around, scamper back to the obstacle, climb over it again, and return to the starting position. To make things a little more interesting, they were asked to support the pillow between their bodies at all times (no hands, arms, or teeth allowed) and had only sixty seconds to complete the course. So that no one finished disappointed, the research team removed participants' watches and pretended that everyone completed the task in the allotted time.

> The pleasure which we most rarely experience gives us greatest delight.
>
> *Epictetus*

The couples in the other group were asked to do something far more mundane, like roll a ball to a designated spot in the center of the room. The partner was asked to watch from the side of the room and eventually asked to change places for the same task. Yawn.

At the end of the experiment, all of the couples completed several questionnaires, rating, for example, the degree to which their partner made them "tingle" and "burst with happiness." Was there a difference between the two groups? You bet. The couples who conquered the foam obstacle were far more loving toward one another than those who had completed the ball-rolling task. They actually found one another more attractive than the other group. The Velcro couples made far more positive comments and were happier than the ball rollers.

> Marriage is an adventure, not an achievement.
>
> *David A. Seamands*

Thank about that. Just a few minutes of a new and fun joint activity appeared to have worked wonders in boosting happiness and intimacy.[5]

We have no problem believing these results. You can probably imagine the conversation over dinner we had following our flying trapeze class together. We were both animated and laughing harder than we had in a good while:

"I didn't think that guy was going to catch you."

"I know. I was so nervous I could barely focus on what I was supposed to do. Did you see his face when I let go of the bar?"

The experience jostled us out of our routine. You know the feeling. You're excited. Adrenaline is pumping. Your brain is high on dopamine. You feel happy in love. In fact, if you were to undergo a brain scan following the moment of euphoria, you'd see that the area of the brain that controls fear, and another region involved in negative emotions, would be closed down. It's the same thing that happened early in your relationship when you were dating and falling head over heels for each other. New and exciting experiences together reignite those loving feelings and tap into those same "happy places" in your brain. In other words, trying new things makes you happy together. You might say that trying new things is the love drug for married couples.

How to Try New Things Together

Holiday Inn used to run an ad: "The best surprise is no surprise at all." Really? Do you want to visit a new place and find it to be just like someplace you've been before? If not, you're ready for adventure. Here are some new tips on reinvigorating your relationship with some adventure and a few surprises. As always, lean into the tips you think will work best for you.

Become Fanatics Together

"My husband, Edward, is devoted to hawks and especially to the golden eagles that are returning to our part of Georgia," said Barbara Brown Taylor, a professor at Piedmont College in rural Georgia. "Driving down the highway with him can be a test of nerves as he cranes over the steering wheel to peer at the wing feathers of a particularly large bird." Her husband, like any bird enthusiast, wants to know, is it an eagle or just a turkey vulture? In fact, as Barbara said, Edward *has* to know, even if it means weaving down the road for a while, or running off it from time to time. "My view," she continued, "is a bit different: 'Keep your eyes on the road!' I yell at him. 'Who cares what it is? I'll buy you a bird book; I'll even buy you a bird—just watch where you're going.'"

> Melt down two pasts into a single now and gladly risk two futures on one vow.
>
> *Stanly Wiersma*

A couple of summers ago, Barbara and Edward's schedules kept them apart for two months and she thought she'd get a break from hawks. "Instead I began to see them everywhere," she said, "looping through the air, spiraling in rising thermals, hunkered down in the tops of trees. Seeing them, really seeing them, for the first time in my life, I understood that I was not seeing them with my own eyes but with Edward's eyes. He was not there, so I was seeing them for him."

Barbara couldn't wait to connect with her husband and tell him of the hawks she'd seen. Barbara was becoming a bird fanatic like her husband. And when husband and wife share a passion, whether it's birds, Beethoven, or breakfast, it builds a bond that heightens happiness together.

But what if you can't lean into a passion one of you already has? That's when it's time for something completely different. That's when it's time to become fanatics together. How? By choosing a brand-new passion for anything that you both agree on. It might be museums, ball games, antiquing, motorcycles, gardening, painting, cars, genealogy, scuba diving, woodworking, photography, tennis, or anything else that comes to mind. A fanatic is someone with extreme and uncritical enthusiasm or zeal for something. What could the two of you be fanatical about? It doesn't have to be forever. It could be for a year or even a summer.

We have some friends who have been married about twenty years, and they took this tip to heart. They decided to become fanatics about roller coasters. They'd ridden a few early on in their lives, but they decided to do something a little whacky—and got their two teenage kids involved as well. They saw a documentary on roller coasters that sparked the idea. They bought a book about some of the most famous roller coasters in America. They made a list of ten roller coasters they wanted to ride—including the tallest, the fastest, the oldest, and the longest. They planned their vacations around riding them. In short, they became roller coaster fanatics. And they loved it. Mention nearly any coaster by name and they can tell you all about it, even if they haven't taken the ride—yet.

So whether it's bird watching, roller coasters, or anything else, consider becoming fanatics together—at least for a season—about something that might even be surprising.

Heat Up Some Hot Monogamy

"You want me to put what where?" That question, from either spouse, is enough to stunt the progress of any couple's lovemaking. But if it's been a long time since you've tried a new sexual position, if you've settled in on a "standard position" like most married couples do after a few years, it may be time to shake it up.

Perhaps you've even forgotten that there are numerous options available to you. Let's see: there's the Criss-Cross, the Down Dog, the Slow Climb, the Giddy-Up, the Spoon, the Pinwheel, the Mermaid, and the ever elusive Spider Web. We're not confident we even know what most of these are, but we do know that if your sex life is putting you to sleep, a new position will wake you both up. You don't need to check out a copy of the Karma Sutra. There are numerous wholesome helps in this area. Kevin Leman covers the basics of various sexual positions in his book *Sheet Music*, as do Cliff and Joyce Penner in their book *The Gift of Sex*.

> You've got to ask! Asking is, in my opinion, the world's most powerful—and neglected—secret to success and happiness.
>
> *Percy Ross*

Here's the point: there's a powerful tendency in an enduring marriage to favor the predictable over the unpredictable. Yet without an element of uncertainty we reduce our sexual anticipation and excitement.

Now, we need to put forth a major qualifier on sexual positions. When it's a mind-blowing, bed-rattling orgasm you're after, keeping it simple is typically best. Sure, wild, crazy, never-knew-my-body-could-bend-that-way sex might keep your love life exciting, but if the goal of the moment is to break pleasure records, you can't neglect the basics.

Oh, and it might be time to think outside the bed. Who said your sex life is limited to your mattress? If you want to spice up your lovemaking, find a new location. Just like a new position increases anticipation and excitement on occasion, so does a unique sexual locale. For example, has it been a while since you've enjoyed sudsy sex in your bathtub or shower together? Or how about steaming up the windows of your car after pulling into the garage after a dinner out—even as a precursor to going to your bedroom? You get the idea. And you've had the thoughts. So why not invite your spouse to a new space for a little adventure and a literal change of pace.

Make New Friends Together

We were five couples who hadn't even met each other before but we were all in the same boat—with one of the spouses in each couple starting a six-year doctoral program. Somehow we got together for a little mixer at one of our apartments. We were all new to Los Angeles and compared notes on where to shop for groceries,

> Here's to having an excellent adventure and may the stopping never start.
>
> *Jason Mraz*

restaurants to try, and so on. Then somebody said, "Maybe we should start a small group that meets every week." And we did. For six years we rotated through each other's little homes and met for no other reason than to be friends—together as couples. And it made all the difference. We commiserated and celebrated experiences together. And knowing we had this safety net of friends together couldn't help but lift our spirits and boost happiness.

"Of all the means to insure happiness throughout the whole life, by far the most important is the acquisition of friends," said Greek philosopher Epicurus. And he wrote those words somewhere around 300 BC—long before any social scientists were around to research his claim. But today we have a mountain of studies that reveal just how accurate Epicurus was.

In 1937 a researcher at Harvard University began a study on what factors contribute to human well-being and happiness. The research team selected 268 male Harvard students who seemed healthy and well-adjusted to be part of what is called a longitudinal study, which means that the researchers would study the lives of these men not just at one point in time, but rather over a period of time. In this case, the period of time has been extraordinary: seventy-two years. With that many years of perspective, the study gives a comprehensive viewpoint on what has affected the level of health and happiness of men over a lifetime.

The study has tracked an array of factors, including standard measurable items like physical exercise, cholesterol levels, marital status, the use of alcohol, smoking, education levels, and weight, but also more subjective psychological factors such as how a person employs defense mechanisms to deal with the challenges of life.

Over the period of seventy-two years, several men have directed the research. For the last forty-two years, the director has been psychiatrist George Vaillant. Recently someone asked Dr. Vaillant, age seventy-eight, what he had learned about human health and happiness from his years of poring over the data on these 268 men. You would expect a complex answer from a Harvard social scientist, but his secret to happiness was breathtakingly simple: "The only thing that really matters in life are your relationships to other people."[6]

Study after study has underscored this point. The most salient fact is this: people with the highest levels of happiness have irrefutably strong ties to friends and are committed to sharing time with them. And couples that have shared friendships—where both members in the couple enjoy the friendship of the other couple—are the happiest couples on the planet.[7]

> Happiness consists in activity. It is a running stream, not a stagnant pool.
>
> *John Mason Good*

Of course, finding and building friendships with other couples can be an adventure. So here's our challenge to you: if your circle of friends as a couple is a little small or nonexistent, start a small group with other couples. Simply wrangle two to four other couples you'd like to get to know and invite them to your place. You can make it informal with no agenda other than being together, or you can set it up for a brief study of a book or even to watch a program. The goal is to be intentional about building your social web of connection with other couples and doing a bit of life together with them. Is it a little risky? Sure. That's why it's an adventure.

Buy Experiences—Not Things

A national survey asked people to think of an object or experience that they had bought with the aim of increasing their happiness and then to rate how well it worked. An example of buying things might be a new smartphone, a new sweater, or a piece of furniture. Buying an experience might be going out for a meal, attending a concert, or booking a vacation.

The survey researchers did a second study where they randomly divided people into two groups, asked one group to think about an object they had recently bought and the other to describe an experience they purchased. The results from both studies clearly indicated that in terms of short- and long-term happiness, buying experiences make people happier than buying products.[8]

Why is this? Researchers believe it's due to our memories becoming a little distorted over time.[9] We tend to edit out parts of a trip that aren't so happy, like a cramped airplane ride, and remember mostly the blissful moment of relaxing on the beach. Experiences tend to get better with age. The goods we buy, on the other hand, tend to lose their luster by becoming old, worn out, and outdated. We spend more time overall contemplating our experiences rather than material purchases. Plus experiences promote one of the most effective happiness-inducing behaviors we have as couples: spending time with each other.[10]

So if you're itching to buy some happiness, spend your hard-earned cash on experiences. Go out for a nice meal. Go to the theater or bungee jump. Buy an adventure rather than an object.

A Final Thought on Trying New Things Together

Remember the 1997 blockbuster film *Titanic*? The epic romance on the ill-fated voyage shows how Jack Dawson wins the affection of a wealthy young woman named Rose Bukater. Although Rose turns Jack away at first, she yearns inside for someone to break her free of her dismal life.

In perhaps the most famous scene of the movie, Rose has decided to give their romance a chance and has sought out Jack on the bow of the ship. When he sees her change of heart towards him, he reaches out to her and says, "Take my hand." He asks her not to speak but to close her eyes, and then he leads her to the very bow of the ship. He has her stand up on the railing, while he holds her steady. He asks Rose, "Do you trust me?"

She responds, "I trust you."

The scene radiates as the sunset streaks the background. As Jack stretches out her arms over the bow and tells her to open her eyes, she's overwhelmed by the beauty of the waters and the sunset before her. All she can say is, "I'm flying!"

Rose is being rescued from a predictable and passionless life and invited to pursue something more. That's the feeling of excitement and adventure, to say the least. In fact, it's an over-the-top Hollywood adventure on top of incredible romance—everything necessary for an epic film to win eleven Academy Awards.

Thankfully, you don't have to sail on a doomed and sinking ship to create your epic adventure. Whenever you try new things together, you're already on your way to bucking boredom and boosting happiness. Trying new things helps you fall in love again and again. And after all, "A successful marriage requires falling in love many times," says Germaine Greer, "always with the same person."

For Reflection

1. What is likely to keep you in your comfort zone and prevent you from trying new things together? More important, what's it going to take to get you up and stepping outside your comfort zone?

2. What do you make of the study descried in the chapter where pairs of couples were linked by Velcro to perform a novel task of simply completing an obstacle course? Are you surprised that something as basic as this could elevate their happiness together? Why or why not?

3. From the tips and ideas in this chapter to help you try something new, which one are you most likely to try and when? Be specific.

5 Dream a Dream

Hope is itself a species of happiness, and, perhaps, the chief happiness which this world affords.

Samuel Johnson

MAYBE YOU'VE SEEN THE Pixar animated movie *Up*, depicting the last adventure of a seventy-eight-year-old balloon salesman named Carl Fredricksen. If you have children in your home it's pretty much a requirement, at least in our circles.

One of the most important elements of the film is Carl's status as a widower. His wife, Ellie, was more than the love of his life—she was the spark and spirit as well. But because the story begins some time after Ellie's death, the filmmakers had to find a way to communicate the depth and meaning of Carl and Ellie's relationship in a way that didn't take away from the main plotline. Their solution was a short vignette at the beginning of the movie that quickly and powerfully details the story of their lives. There is no dialogue, only a series of brief scenes perfectly complemented by a musical score. But the result speaks volumes about the thrilling ups and terrible downs in a lifetime of marriage. Mostly, however, it speaks of the couple's dream.

The vignette starts with a brief glimpse of Carl and Ellie's wedding day and then moves to their first home and first jobs—Carl as a balloon salesman at a zoo and Ellie as a zookeeper. The couple race up a grassy hill together, then look up at the sky and imagine pictures forming in the clouds. Then the clouds are all shaped like babies, and then Carl and Ellie are painting a nursery together. It's an idyllic look at young love and marriage.

> An aim in life is the only future worth finding.
>
> *Robert Louis Stevenson*

But this isn't an idyllic life. The scene shifts to Carl and Ellie in a hospital room with prenatal diagrams on the walls. A doctor is talking and gesturing. Ellie is weeping into her hands. Next Carl comforts his wife by reminding her of an old dream they shared when they were children—travelling to a place called Paradise Falls together. Rejuvenated, Ellie creates a dream jar labeled "Paradise Falls," and into the jar goes all of the young couple's spare money.

Again, however, life happens. First their car pops a tire. Then Carl visits the hospital. Then a tree falls and damages the roof of their home. Each of these inconveniences necessitates that the dream jar be smashed and the money spent. Soon Carl and Ellie have gray in their hair. And in a flash they become elderly.

Near the end of the vignette, Carl remembers their dream of visiting Paradise Falls, and he purchases two tickets from a travel agency. But Ellie collapses on her way back up the grassy hill of their youth. We see her in a hospital bed, with Carl holding her hand and kissing her forehead. Then we see Carl sitting alone at the front of a church. He holds a solitary balloon in his hand.

As the vignette closes we clearly see that Carl and Ellie loved each other deeply. Their relationship was fun, tragic, tender, and filled with hope. They had a dream.

And chances are you do too. Every newlywed couple begins their relationship with dreams. Unfortunately, the strum and strain of life has a way of getting in front of our dreams and our proverbial "dream jar" is at risk of getting smashed. We've got to tend to our dreams before it's too late. And that's exactly what we'll help you do in this chapter. Why? Because following your dreams is a critical ingredient of being happy together. But be forewarned: all dreams are not created equal. Some make us happier than others—much happier, as we're about to see.

Defining Dreaming

Marriage is the one place where we have the potential to create a world that is to our own liking. Why? Because *we* determine our dreams. It's up to us to craft a vision for what is possible in our home and relationship. And that's exactly what a dream is: a vision of the imagination that is strongly desired and hoped for. A dream entails a goal or a purpose that gets us to a place we long to be—a place where we will be happier. In fact, you might be surprised to learn that the Old English root of the word *dream* literally means "mirth" or "joy."

> It doesn't hurt to be optimistic. You can always cry later.
>
> *Lucimar Santos de Lima*

You can't dream without optimism and hope. They are the double doors to happiness. When we were in graduate school together, one of our favorite professors was noted author and scholar Lewis Smedes. He said hope is made up of three ingredients: First, there's a desire for something to be different. Second is the belief that it can happen. And third is the worry that it won't. That's the rub. Our beliefs need convincing. We fear the possibility that what we hope for may not happen, and the greater our fears, the less hope we have. That's why human hope—dreaming of our future—involves risk. It's also why too many couples never dare to dream a dream.

How Dreaming Boosts Your Happiness

Dreaming brings together two super-boosters of happiness: optimism and control. Either one of these traits is enough to measurably increase a person's life satisfaction, but when you dream a dream together you tap into the power of both at the same time.

> "What day is it?"
> "It's today," squeaked Piglet.
> My favorite day," said Pooh."
>
> *A. A. Milne*

Consider optimism. Few traits are more strongly linked to personal happiness than seeing the glass half full as opposed to half empty. Hundreds, if not thousands, of studies show that optimism leads to better consequences than pessimism does.[1] Optimistic people have been shown to achieve more, build stronger relationships, and have better health. Optimists are also superior at deflecting depression and bouncing back from hardship.

Dr. Dennis Charney, the dean of Mount Sinai School of Medicine, examined approximately 750 Vietnam War veterans who were held as prisoners of war for six to eight years. Tortured and kept in solitary confinement, these 750 men were remarkably resilient. Unlike many fellow veterans, they did not develop depression or posttraumatic stress disorder after their release, even though they endured extreme conditions. What was their secret? After extensive interviews and tests, Charney found ten characteristics that set them apart. At the top of the list was optimism. They held out hope and could picture life beyond their suffering. Their optimism pulled them through.

Optimists believe what Victor Hugo wrote in *Les Misérables*:

> A pessimist is one who makes difficulties of his opportunities and an optimist is one who makes opportunities of his difficulties.
>
> *Harry Truman*

"Even the darkest night will end and the sun will rise." But optimism does more than bolster resilience and fight against depression. It elevates happiness.

Dreaming a dream also involves personal control. Happy people believe they have a lot to say about their destiny. "Hell is to drift, heaven is to steer," said George Bernard Shaw. Those that drift feel helpless, as if nothing they choose to do affects what happens to them. Everything is up to luck or fate. By contrast, people who dream a dream, who see a vision for what their life can be, take action to make it so. Dreaming galvanizes action to make things better.

Summarizing the University of Michigan's nationwide surveys, Angus Campbell said: "Having a strong sense of controlling one's life is a more dependable predictor of positive feelings of well-being than any of the objective condition of life we have considered." In other words, more vital to happiness than a great job, a perfect marriage, making good money, or having good health is having control over what you do and where you go. It's having influence over your life's direction. In short, it's having freedom to follow your dreams.

The 15 percent of the population who feel the most control over their lives have "extraordinarily positive feelings of happiness," says Campbell. Among these people, three in five—double the national average—report being very happy.

"Hope is passion for what is possible," said Søren Kierkegaard. And what is possible for the person who dreams is more happiness.

What's Your Dream Quotient?

Few actions do more to insure that our marriage doesn't hit a slump than dreaming a dream together.

T F We have talked at length about our dreams for our relationship and our life together. I can recall where we were and much of what we said.

T F We've talked about our dreams together, if only for a moment, in the past month.

T F We have written down our dreams and I know where to find them.

T F We have a bucket list of cool things we'd like to do at some point in our lives.

T F We have broken our most important dreams into a set of achievable goals.

T F I'm optimistic about achieving our dreams together.

T F Some of our dreams may not be what people would call "fun," but they are very meaningful to us.

T F I can easily picture our marriage twenty-five years from now and I know what I'd like it to be like.

T F I feel like for the most part we are in charge of the direction our life is taking.

T F Thinking about our future together is energizing to me.

Making Sense of Your Score

How many of the above statement are true for you? The higher the number, the more likely you are to be on your way to dreaming dreams together. Of course, if your score was lower than you like, don't be discouraged. You're going to find a lot of help in this chapter.

What Dreaming Together
Does for Your Relationship

"Sometimes late at night, Tony and I talk about how our lives will be when our three children are grown up and out of the house," says author Charlotte Latvala. "We'll travel. I'll write novels; he'll make cabinetry in his neglected basement workshop—we'll have a new and exciting life together. I'm not sure how much of this will happen, but talking about it makes us feel close."

And it does—for all of us. Talking together about how we see the future is essential for boosting happiness in marriage. When we don't, we increase the odds for failure on all fronts. Tom Lee, a professor of marriage and family studies at Utah State University, recently completed a survey of fourteen hundred married people. One of the findings was that couples who regularly discuss their long-range plans are more likely to stay happily married. "If you have a long-term view, you realize that the daily ups and downs don't mean as much," he says. "Talking about your shared future communicates, 'I plan on being here.' The message is that there are plenty of good times yet to come."

Dreaming a dream together doesn't just elevate happiness when you talk about it, however. Research reveals that simply being close to your spouse can cause you to be more optimistic in your outlook, more hopeful and less intimidated by a challenge.

In a series of studies carried out by Simone Schnall from the University of Plymouth, people

> When we dream alone is it only a dream, but when we dream together it is the beginning of a new reality.
>
> *Friedensreich Hundertwasser*

were taken to the bottom of a hill and asked to estimate how steep it was and therefore how difficult it would be to climb.[2] When they were accompanied by a spouse or friend, their estimates were about 15 percent lower than when they were on their own, and even just thinking about a spouse when looking at the hill made it seem far more surmountable.

In other words, dreaming together makes your dream more achievable than it would be dreaming alone. It stirs optimism and empowers action. Happy marriages are built on dreams and visions.

> We are, each of us angels with only one wing; and we can only fly by embracing one another.
>
> *Luciano de Crescenzo*

How to Dream Together

Chances are you already have dreams you're dreaming together. The tips in this section will help you hone them. They may also help you to dream new dreams together. Lean into the tips that are most helpful.

Take a Mental Time Trip

Dreaming begins with what may be the most extraordinary of human talents: mental time travel. That is, the ability to move back and forth through time and space in your mind. And you're most likely to discover your dreams when you visit your future. So our first tip is straight to the point: see your future.

Imagine yourself years down the road in as much detail as possible. Can you see your face in your senior years? If not, research at Stanford University wants to help. In fact, they call it a game changer for anyone dreaming about and planning for their future. And they're not kidding around. They have developed software that instantly ages your image and they plan to bring it to your company's HR department.[3]

As part of their research, students were placed in front of a computer screen that either showed them as they were or as they might look in thirty years. They were then asked what they would do with one thousand dollars given to them at that moment. Those who had seen their future self-allocated twice as much of the windfall to a retirement account.[4]

> In dreams and in love there are no impossibilities.
>
> *Janos Arnay*

Unless you have the equivalent of this electronic time machine, we simply ask you to close your eyes and imagine what your life and your marriage look like in the future. What do they look like one year from now? Five years from now? Ten? Twenty-five?

Nearly a decade ago we'd been married about seventeen years and we did this very exercise. And one of the things we envisioned together was living in downtown Seattle (not in a suburb). Six years ago we made that move and we've never looked back. The vision was fraught with challenges, but it's been one of the best things we've ever done for our family. And it happened because we took a mental time trip together.

So picture the life and love you see for yourselves. Talk to each other about your visions and what you see. If you are open to hearing each other, this simple exercise will generate a terrific conversation and set the stage for dreaming together.

Release Your Fear Factor

It takes courage to envision your future. Some fear it sets the stage for failure. In fact, some people believe the secret to happiness is low expectations. "If I expect as little as possible, I won't be hurt," Susan Sontag famously wrote in her diary. The fear of failure is so strong for some it keeps them from dreaming. The thinking goes like this: if we are never disappointed when things don't work out and are pleasantly surprised when things go well, we will be happy. It may sound like a good theory—but it's wrong. Research makes it clear. Whatever the outcome, whether we succeed or we fail, people with high expectations tend to feel better.[5] At the end of the day, how we feel when we fail at a task or win an award depends mostly on how we interpret the experience.

A common saying among mountaineers is this: it's not the mountain that stops you, it's the pebble in your shoe. Is fear of failure the pebble in your shoe? Take it out. How? By accepting that failure is part of the journey. Every dreamer has setbacks. As Thomas Edison said, "I failed my way to success." Don't let fear hobble your attempt to climb the mountain of your dreams. "Far better is it to dare mighty things, to win glorious triumphs, even though checkered by failure," said Theodore Roosevelt, "than to rank with those poor spirits who neither enjoy nor suffer much, because they live in a gray twilight that knows not victory nor defeat."

Build a Bucket List

In January of 2008, a film starring Jack Nicholson and Morgan Freeman launched a phrase into everyday parlance that got people talking. *Bucket List* follows two

> Never let the fear of striking out get in your way.
> *George Herman "Babe" Ruth*

terminally ill men on a road trip with a wish list for things to do before they "kick the bucket." The two men go skydiving together, drive a

Shelby Mustang, eat dinner at Chevre d'Or in France, ride motorcycles on the Great Wall of China, and so on.

The film got a lot of people thinking about their bucket list, including the two of us. We made a list that includes, in part:

- an African safari
- hang gliding
- visiting Mount Rushmore
- eating tacos at Mi Tierra's in San Antonio
- snorkeling off the Amalfi Coast
- attending the National Finals Rodeo
- taking our boys to Fenway Park in Boston
- sleeping in an ancient castle
- sailing the San Juan Islands
- attending the Indy 500
- walking part of the Great Wall of China (which we did two years ago—no motorbikes needed)

We used this exercise of building a bucket list to focus on the frivolous, for the most part. Our list is long and nothing was discarded. It's just a list of dreams that sound fun to us. Some random wishes. Some lifelong desires.

> A dream is not something that you wake up from, but something that wakes you up.
>
> *Charlie Hedges*

A bucket list is an attempt to make life memorable and it's consistent with what researchers call *peak-end theory*, which holds that what people remember most when reminiscing together are their pleasurable peaks in their lives.[6] In other words, it's not the duration of a vacation that makes it memorable, it's the peaks. Few peaks, few memories (or at least not very crisp ones). So if you haven't made a bucket list together, give it some thought. And start making memories.

Oh, one more thing: don't fall into the trap of making a list of things you think will impress others. Make it for yourselves.

> And in the end, it's not the years in your life that count. It's the life in your years.
>
> *Abraham Lincoln*

When you start to play the look-how-cool-we-are game you miss out on the fun and happiness your dream list can offer.

Dream a Dream with Meaning

The English word *wisdom* is derived from an old Anglo-Saxon word meaning "to see." And in Greek it means "clear." Wisdom is what enables us to see the big picture. Wisdom ensures that our dreaming is about more than fun. Wise dreamers dream *meaningful* dreams.

People who strive for something significant are far happier than those who don't have meaningful dreams or aspirations.[7] After all, satisfying a fun desire increases happiness for a bit but is largely irrelevant to achieving a meaningful dream. Just ask any couple who has adopted a child, worked hard to get healthy, volunteered at a local shelter, poured themselves into raising honorable children, given sacrificially to a relief fund, hosted an exchange student, mentored newlywed couples, cared lovingly for a aging parent, volunteered for a youth mission trip, or simply devoted themselves to building a strong and vibrant marriage for their family.

Researchers Ed Diener and Robert Biswas-Diener make it clear that dreams are about more than pleasure: "As humans, we actually require a sense of meaning to thrive." Harvard's resident happiness professor, Tal Ben-Shahar, agrees, "Happiness lies at the intersection between pleasure and meaning. Whether at work or at home, the goal is to engage in activities that are both personally significant and enjoyable."

The deeper our hopes and dreams, the more satisfying and meaningful is our life together. The realization of a shallow hope (buying a new car) simply reveals how vapid the hope was to begin with. It's short lived and thin as vapor, as the Bible says.[8] And if we keep holding out false hope that it is going to truly fulfill us, only to encounter continual disappointment, we will eventually shake our fist to the heavens like the writer of Ecclesiastes, saying, "Everything is futile."[9]

> Dream as if you'll live forever, live as if you'll die today.
>
> *James Dean*

So how could there be a hope that does *not* disappoint? Because it is a hope that is carried by faith.[10] And faith changes everything. "Faith is being sure of what we hope for," as the apostle Paul said.[11] It moves worry to the backstage of hope. Faith emboldens our beliefs and expectations with confidence. Faith can make us fearless. "Hope is hearing the melody of the future," said Rubem Alves. "Faith is to dance to it."

How does faith do this mystical work? By giving us an eternal perspective. People of faith and wisdom look at life differently. Hope-filled optimism about our future, when bolstered by faith, moderates our anxiety. We look at life through a bigger lens. Viewing life's problems through the big lens of the future helps put in perspective today's struggles.

James Pennebaker, a psychological researcher at the University of Texas in Austin, has found that people who find meaning in adversity are ultimately healthier in the long run than those who do not. In a study, he asked people to write about the darkest, most traumatic, experience of their lives for four days in a row for a period of fifteen minutes each day. Analyzing their writing, Pennebaker noticed that the people who benefited most from the exercise were trying to derive meaning from the trauma. They were probing into the causes and consequences of the adversity and, as a result, eventually grew wiser about it. A year later, their medical records showed that the meaning-makers went to the doctor and hospital fewer times than people in the control condition, who wrote about a nontraumatic event. People who used the exercise to vent, by contrast, received no health benefits.

Faith turns hope into a certainty that suffering will make sense even when our earthly perspective can only see it as senseless. In other words, when pain cuts us to the core and hardships punch us in the solar plexus, faith is responsible for keeping our hope alive. Faith draws us to dream of making a difference. It propels us to aspire higher for our future and live honorable lives together. Happiness without meaning is vapid. But meaning without happiness is impossible.

> I am not good at noticing when I'm happy, except in retrospect.
>
> *Tana French*

Keep Hope Alive

A team of researchers recently studied what they called *hope induction* on the effect of fulfilling our dreams.[12] For about fifteen minutes, research participants were asked to think of an important goal and to imagine how they might achieve it. A comparison condition asked participants to read a home organization book for about fifteen minutes. All participants were then asked to immerse their nondominant hand in a bucket of ice water for as long as they could (up to five minutes). This is a standard measure of pain tolerance, and it is painful but not harmful.

Participants receiving the brief hope induction kept their hand immersed for about 150 seconds. Those in the comparison condition, low on hope, kept their hand immersed for only ninety seconds. Hope, the researchers concluded, did not affect reports on how painful the experience was, but it did increase the ability to tolerate it.

No doubt about it, hope helps you achieve your goals and realize your dream. So how do you keep hope alive? Experts say the answer is found in talking about your dream. Often. Dreaming together is not something you check off your to-do list. It's not a one-and-done proposition. Dreaming together is organic and evolving. It's a conversation topic that never ends.

> A vision is not just a picture of what could be; it is an appeal to our better selves, a call to become something more.
>
> *Rosabeth Moss Kanter*

If it helps, make a *dream board* (or use an app) where you collect images and pictures that remind you of your dream. If you want to bicycle in France someday, put that on the board. If you want to help build a house for Habitat for Humanity, put that up. For some couples, a dream board is a perfect catalyst for conversing—and keeping hope alive in the process.

Get S.M.A.R.T.

Ask most people if they have goals for their life and they'll say, "Of course." Ask them if they've written them down and they'll scratch their head. Does it matter? You bet. In a study done at Yale University, researchers found that people who wrote down their goals achieved them 97 percent more often than those who did not.[13] Incredible, right? So here's our suggestion: set aside a few minutes to not only talk about your dreams, but write them down. Use a legal pad, a notebook, or your computer—whatever works. Why? Because putting your dreams in writing clarifies your thinking. It forces you to be more specific. It may help you prioritize them. And the more specific your dreams, the more likely you are to outline the goals that will help you achieve them.

In fact, breaking down a dream that envisions some aspect of your future into step-by step goals is essential. It's too unwieldy if you don't. One of the dreams we wrote down as a couple a few years back was to write a book that would be a *New York Times* bestseller. We'd written several books but never made that coveted list (every author's dream). Well, it's one thing to dream about that, and another to formulate goals that will make it happen. But that's just what we did. And we used the time-tested S.M.A.R.T. method. This means we made sure our goals were Specific, Measurable, Achievable, Realistic, and Time-Sensitive.

You might be curious to know if our dream came true. It did. Just last year. In fact, our book *The Hour That Matters Most* ended up at number one on the list. And it would have likely never happened if we didn't write it down, talk about it often, and get S.M.A.R.T. about setting our goals.

Don't Dream Dumb

We'd be remiss if we didn't mention that too much of a good thing, when it comes to optimism about your dreams, can be dumb. Researchers call it *foolish optimism*. It's part of why people save too little for retirement, thinking, "Things will work out somehow."

Scientists have long wondered how foolish optimism manages to survive, especially since one of the key tenets of how the brain learns is that we continuously update our knowledge in light of experience and new information. Now, in the first study of its kind, neuroscientists have pinpointed the brain circuits that underlie unrealistic optimism.[14] What they found is that the frontal lobes, which analyze information, basically look the other way when unrealistic optimists receive information that undercuts one of their rosy beliefs.

Think of a toddler covering her ears and chanting, "*Nyah, nyah, I can't hear you!*" to an adult reprimanding her. The necessary data processing was simply "not going on in the high optimists when they received negative information," says researcher Tali Sharot. It seems that "we pick and choose the information that we listen to. The more optimistic we are, the less likely we are to be influenced by negative information about the future."

Dr. Sharot is still a fan of optimism, just not foolish optimism that doesn't consider the facts or receive input from others. In other words, healthy optimism sees the glass as half full but it also takes precautions. It believes we will stay healthy, for example, but gets medical insurance anyway—just in case.

The recipe for dreams that lead to happiness includes a mix of ample optimism to provide hope, a dash of pessimism to prevent complacency, and enough realism to discriminate those things we can control from those we cannot. It's what theologian Reinhold Niebuhr offered in his "The Serenity Prayer": "O God, give us grace to accept with serenity the things that cannot be changed, courage to change the things which should be changed, and the wisdom to distinguish the one from the other."

A Final Thought
on Dreaming Together

Not far from our home in Seattle sits a little one-story house that has become a local landmark. Edith Macefield moved into the cottage when the street was lined with a row of cute picket-fence homes. But that was then. Fifty years later, Edith was still living in the same house when everything around her had changed. Developers had acquired the entire block of real estate to build a shopping center. The only piece they still needed was Edith's house. But Edith had no interest in selling the sliver of land, valued at one hundred thousand dollars, that she'd lived on most of her life– not even when the developers offered her a million dollars to move out.[15]

Today, a few years after Edith's death in 2008, the cottage is surrounded on three sides by a five-story complex. That's why in May of 2009, Disney heard about Edith and tied balloons to the roof of her house, as a promotional tie-in to their film *Up*. The seventy-eight-year-old balloon salesman named Carl was faced with the same situation, living as an aging widower surrounded by a looming development.

Almost every time we drive by Edith's home, which it at least once a week, we can't help but let it remind us that we want to live out the dreams we dream. We don't want to run the risk of smashing our dream jar and never fulfilling the dreams we aspire to. That's why we work to keep hope alive as we dream our dreams together. As Orison Marden said, "There is no medicine like hope, no incentive so great, and no tonic so powerful as expectation of something better tomorrow."

For Reflection

1. Do you believe that dreaming a dream together, making plans, and setting goals about the future makes couples happier? Much happier? What's a specific example from your own relationship that demonstrates this fact?

2. Do you find it easier to come up with a fun bucket list of dreams you'd like to realize or more meaningful dreams that go deeper than just having fun? Why? Examples?

3. How does your personal faith factor into your dreams together? How does it compliment your hope for a brighter and better future you can create together?

6 Celebrate Each Other

There is no such thing in anyone's life as an unimportant day.

Alexander Woollcott

HAROLD COURTED HER FOR three years, walking her to the theater on warm nights and bringing flowers and chocolates to her uncle's store where she was the cashier. But sixty-five years after she said "I do," Harold is still trying to woo Marion—even as Alzheimer's disease has erased most of her memory. It shut down her command of the family piano and her ability to make the brisket Harold loved so much. The disease robbed her of even remembering her husband most of the time. But while she doesn't recognize him, Harold says, he still recognizes Marion.

That's why every week Harold visits Marion at the center where she receives round-the-clock care from professionals. He comes into her room with decorations, party hats, a little birthday sign with her name on it, and two cupcakes from her favorite bakery.

Harold asks Marion: "Do you know what day it is?"

"No," Marion says. "What day is it?"

"It's your birthday and we're going to celebrate," Harold tells her with a big grin.

A couple of Marion's nurses know the weekly drill and join Harold as they sing "Happy Birthday" and then applaud as Marion blows out the candle on her buttercream cupcake.

"Oh, my, this is the best cupcake I've ever had," is Marion's typical response.

"I thought you'd like it, sweetie," Harold tells her.

He gives her a sweet kiss on the forehead, tells her she's beautiful, and hands her a little gift to open—sometimes a piece of jewelry he gave her years earlier and sometimes a familiar photo of the two of them. Whatever it is, Marion is opening it for the first time and delights in the celebration.

So does Harold. After they eat their cupcakes Harold holds her hand for a few minutes and reminisces for a bit or listens to music they both enjoy. But mostly he celebrates Marion and the life they shared for more than six decades. "I still picture her as the cashier, and I can't believe how blessed I was to be her husband. We had a great life together."

> When we recall the past, we usually find that it is the simplest things—not the great occasions—that in retrospect give off the greatest glow of happiness.
>
> *Bob Hope*

When asked why he celebrates her birthday every week, Harold says: "Marion always loved to celebrate birthdays. So why not make every visit I have with her a special celebration?"

Why not, indeed? Few actions mark a moment in time with more positive emotion than celebrating. And that's exactly what this chapter is dedicated to helping the two of you do. But be forewarned: we're not talking about how to throw a great party. The kind of celebrating we're talking about lasts much longer and goes much deeper.

Defining Celebration

Strike up the band. Pop open the champagne. Start the fireworks. When they hear the word *celebration*, most people think of a festive party. After all, we often celebrate birthdays, anniversaries, and holidays like New Year's with parties. As the saying goes, "No one looks back on their life and remembers the nights they got plenty of sleep." Almost everyone likes a good party. But true celebration involves more than cake and confetti.

> Celebration is a human need that we must not, and can not, deny.
>
> *Corita Kent*

If you look up *celebrate* in the dictionary you'll see words like *bless, praise, applaud, commend, compliment, admire,* and *commemorate*. In fact, its Latin origin, *celebrare*, means "to honor." And that's exactly the kind of celebrating we're talking about in this chapter. When it comes to celebrating each other, we're talking about creating special little celebratory moments infused with positive emotion from mutual admiration and honor.

When we treat our spouse with honor we hold them in high respect and celebrate who they are. It takes an average of two years to adapt to the newness of marriage. After that, we start to take each other and the relationship for granted—unless we learn to celebrate each other.

What's Your Celebration Quotient?

How well do you respect, honor, and celebrate your spouse? This little assessment may shed some light for you on your personal inclination to celebrate your partner.

1. When was the last time you felt fortunate to be with your partner—then told him or her?
   A. Past twenty-four hours   B. Past week
   C. Past month   D. Not sure

2. Does your partner feel noticed, admired, and valued by you?
   A. For sure   B. Probably
   C. Hopefully   D. *Cringe*

3. How frequently do you carry out a thoughtful act that shows your partner you were thinking specifically of him or her—expecting nothing in return?
   A. Every day   B. Every week
   C. Every month   D. Not sure

4. Does your spouse feel good about your sex life (frequency and quality)?
   A. I know so   B. I think so
   C. I hope so   D. I'm not sure

5. What's the ratio of positive comments to negative comments you make to your spouse in a typical week?
   A. Way more + than −   B. More + than −
   C. More − than +   D. Way more − than +

6. Would your partner say he or she feels celebrated by you?
   A. For sure   B. Probably
   C. Hopefully   D. Not sure

Tally the number of each letter:

A _____   B _____   C _____   D _____

The more your answers fall toward the A and B side, the better you feel you're doing at celebrating your partner. Of course, this is just a little self-assessment, and it's only as reliable as your honesty in taking it. Regardless of your results, this chapter will help you hone your celebratory skills in your relationship.

How Celebrating Boosts Your Happiness

According to the Nobel Prize-winning scientist Daniel Kahneman, each day we experience approximately twenty thousand moments. A moment is defined as a few seconds in which our brain records an experience. The quality of our days is determined by how our brains recognize and categorize our moments—either as positive, negative, or just neutral. Rarely do we remember neutral moments.

There is no question that the memories of our lives are recorded in terms of positive and negative experiences. Now scientists propose that each day our brains keep track of our positive and negative moments, and the resulting score, the ratio of positive to negative moments, contributes to our overall mood and well-being. The more positive moments, the more happiness we experience.

> Happy marriages begin when we marry the ones we love, and they blossom when we love the ones we marry.
>
> *Tom Mullen*

Frequent positive emotions, feelings of joy, delight, vitality, and celebration, are the very hallmark of happiness. Generally speaking, happy people, regardless of their circumstances, experience positive states more frequently than do their less happy peers. "Happiness consists more in small conveniences or pleasures that occur every day," said Benjamin Franklin, "than in great pieces of good fortune that happen but seldom."

Positive moments, like mini-celebrations, add up over time. That's why happiness experts urge us not to underestimate the positive emotions experienced during ordinary days. Research shows that numerous pleasant mood-boosting moments occurring on a day-to-day or weekly basis, rather than a single big-ticket item like a new car, are what make happiness endure. We adapt to the excitement of a new car and reset our happiness meter before the new car smell even wears off. So don't bank on the big things. The more mini-celebrations we encounter, the more abiding our joy.

What Celebrating
Does for Your Relationship

"There they are," Les said. We were standing in a great hall at a renowned museum in Florence, Italy, and Les was pointing to four huge blocks of marble. "There's the *Captives*," he exclaimed as he grabbed my hand and pulled me along at an energized pace. Les had studied Michelangelo's work in college and these unfinished pieces were on his must-see list at this museum.

Michelangelo intended for each of the blocks to be used on the tomb of Pope Julius. But midway through the project, he decided not to use them and ceased his work. Today anyone traveling to Florence can see the results—a hand protrudes here, a torso of a man there, a leg, a part of a head. None of them are finished. They came to be known as captives, imprisoned or undiscovered. It's as though the figures are trying to break free from their blocks of marble to become what they were intended to be.

Have you ever felt like a part of you was imprisoned or undiscovered in your marriage? Maybe you've felt that your spouse isn't recognizing a part of you. And maybe you're not recognizing all of your spouse. After all, love's work is never finished. But celebrating each other goes a long way in changing all that.

Researchers actually talk about married couples "sculpting" each other. In scientific studies of marriage it's literally called the *Michelangelo effect*. In subtle ways, we are reinforcing patterns in each other via countless

> Celebrate what you want to see more of.
>
> *Thomas J. Peters*

little interactions—positive or negative moments. That sculpting can either reveal more of your partner by celebrating who he or she is or it can hold him or her captive to being virtually unrecognized.

Just as scientists have found that our brains recognize and categorize our moments—either as positive, negative, or just neutral—they've also studied the impact of positive-to-negative interaction ratios in our relationships. They have found that this ratio can be used to predict—with remarkable accuracy—whether or not we succeed in marriage. It all began with noted psychologist John Gottman's exploration of positive-to-negative ratios in marital interactions. Happy relationships, he found, are characterized by a ratio of 5:1. This means that for every negative statement or behavior like criticizing or nagging, there are five positive statements. Gottman calls it the *magic ratio* and he and his colleagues predicted whether seven hundred newlywed couples would stay together or divorce by scoring their positive and negative interactions in one fifteen-minute conversation between each husband and wife. Ten years later, the follow-up revealed that they had predicted divorce with 94 percent accuracy.

Incredible, isn't it? The kind of positivity that engenders celebrating little moments with your spouse by simply saying, "I love you," "I'm so glad I'm married to you," "I'm proud of you," and so on not only increases a couple's happiness, it evokes the best in each other, helping both partner come closer to reaching their best selves. Celebrating each other chips away at whatever is

> You have the power to spread happiness today. A quick note or a kind word is all it takes to bring a smile and lasting memory to someone very special.
>
> *Gary Harrington*

holding us captive. When we recognize, honor, and celebrate each other, we're freed up to be the best person and partner we can be. It's up to us to sculpt the best marriage our love can afford.

How to Celebrate Each Other

If you're ready to bring more honor, admiration, complimenting, recognition, and celebration into your relationship, we want to show you what works. As always, lean into the tips that you think will serve you and your relationship best.

See Something, Say Something

You've heard the phrase. Homeland Security uses it to heighten public awareness for reporting suspicious activity. Well, we want to borrow the phrase to increase your capacity to notice positive moments with your partner.

Let's face it: most marriages have more than enough criticism to go around. Sometimes we blurt out inane comments without a second of thought: "You never hang up your coat" or "You always make us late." Most of us grumble, grouse, and bellyache as if it's part of our genetic makeup. And, in fact, it might be.

Scientists believe that our brain has a built-in negativity bias. In effect, the human brain is like Velcro for negative experiences, but Teflon for positive ones. But here's the good news: these same scientists say we can retrain our brain by seeing the positive and saying something about it.

Neuroscientists have a saying: "Neurons that fire together, wire together." The more you get your neurons firing about positive experiences, the more they'll be wiring up positive neural structures. In other words, you can literally change your hardwiring to be more positive, more upbeat, more celebratory. And it begins with seeing something and saying something whenever your partner does something you like.

If your partner does the laundry (again), say: "I really appreciate you washing our clothes so nicely." That's all. If your spouse picks up the mail, say thanks. It's easy. In short, be on the lookout for any chance you have to pass on a compliment, show appreciation, or let him or her know you noticed something positive they did. These positive comments will ensure your reaching the magic ratio of five positive comments for every negative. They'll also set the stage for celebrating your partner on a deeper level.

> There are a few moments in your life when you are truly and completely happy, and you remember to give thanks. Even as it happens you are nostalgic for the moment, you are tucking it away in your scrapbook.
>
> *David Benioff*

Celebrate Good News Like You Mean It

We can almost hear you thinking: *Well, duh. Of course you celebrate good news.* But not so fast. Research reveals that most of us don't engage with positive news from our partners as much as we do with bad news. We're more inclined to camp out in a conversation when our partner tells about a disappointment than when the topic is upbeat. We focus more on news from our partner about a criticism they received at work, for example, than we do about news of a successful presentation they gave. Weird, right?

And get this: how you respond to good news your partner brings home is a huge indicator of how healthy your relationship is. By the way, the good news doesn't have to be about a job promotion or anything extravagant. It can be as simple as a nice call from an old friend, a meaningful interaction with a colleague over lunch, an insight from something your partner read, or maybe a reached goal they've been working on at the local gym. These are the little pieces of good news. And how you reply to them makes a big difference.

Psychologist Shelly L. Gable at the University of California, Santa Barbara and her colleagues found that couples share positive events with each other surprisingly often. In fact, positive events happen at least three times as often as negative ones for most of us.[1] Unfortunately, when our partner shares the good news we apparently don't often reply with the excitement they'd like to see.[2] We tend to respond in one of three not so encouraging ways: (1) with an obligatory and lifeless comment, (2) by changing the subject, or (3) by quashing the news with a critical remark. But there's a fourth alternative that our partner is eager to experience. Researchers call it an *active-constructive* response that's heartfelt and enthusiastic. This is where you'll find the happiest couples—with high energy and plenty of support.[3] See the following chart:

	HIGH SUPPORT	LOW SUPPORT
HIGH ENERGY	**Encouraging** "That's great news! Tell me more."	**Critical** "That means more stress. I don't envy you."
LOW ENERGY	**Passive** "That's nice."	**Deflective** "Listen to what happened to me."

Four Ways of Responding to Good News in Marriage

Gable and her team recorded married men and women as they took turns discussing a positive and negative event. After each conversation, members of each pair rated how "responded to" (how understood and cared for) they felt by their partner. Separately, the couples evaluated their happiness level in the relationship.

The researchers found that when a partner gave an encouraging response to good news, the "responded to" ratings were higher than they were after a sympathetic response to negative news. The point? How partners reply to good news is a stronger determinant of relationship health and happiness than a partner's reaction to unfortunate news. The reason for this finding, Gable surmised, may be that fixing a problem or dealing with a disappointment—though important for a relationship—may not make a couple feel joy, the currency of a happy marriage.[4]

Even more surprising, Gable's study, and others since, reveal that a low-energy, passive response to good news ("That's nice") or changing the subject ("Did you get the mail?") is as damaging as directly disparaging or criticizing a partner.[5] Yikes! So ask yourself regularly: "What good news has my partner told me today? How can we celebrate it?"

> Stop worrying about the potholes in the road and celebrate the journey.
>
> *Barbara Hoffman*

By the way, just as responding enthusiastically and with encouragement to your partner's good news increases relationship happiness, so does sharing your own positive experiences. In a daily diary study of sixty-seven couples, Gable found that on days when couples reported telling their partner about a happy event, they also reported feeling a stronger tie to their partner and greater security in their relationship.[6]

So if you've been looking for reasons to engage your partner's good news with a few celebratory words, you now have them. And hopefully, so does your partner.

Create an Awe Wall

A young paratrooper was learning to jump, and he was given the following instructions: first, jump when you are told; second, count to ten and pull the ripcord; third, in the unlikely event that it doesn't open, pull the second chute open; and fourth, when you get down, a truck will take you back to base.

The plane ascended up to the proper height, the men started peeling out, and the young paratrooper jumped when told. He counted to ten and pulled the

> When I'm happy inside, that's when I feel most sexy.
> *Anna Kournikova*

cord, but the chute failed to open. He proceeded to the backup plan. The second chute also failed to open. "Oh, boy," he said. "When I get down, I suppose the truck won't be there either."

Let's face it: some people are profoundly pessimistic—a tendency to expect the worst and see the worst. Pessimists have a tougher time celebrating their partner than others. So if you happen to fall into this camp we have a tip especially for you.

Karen Reivich, a research associate at the University of Pennsylvania, sees herself as a recovering pessimist: "Part of my brain is always scanning the horizon for danger." Instead of telling herself that her concerns are unwarranted, Reivich draws on her creativity to counter the dour, gloomy part of her personality. "I've created an 'awe wall' covered with poems, my children's photos, a picture of a lavender farm. And every day I work on it a bit." Reivich says she may add a cartoon that makes her laugh or a picture that inspires her. "It's hard to be basking in all these reminders of wonder and simultaneously be filled with dread."[7]

Reivich and other researchers say that strategies like these, used consistently over time, lead to long-lasting change and a more celebratory spirit. Pessimism atrophies when we deliberately focus on noticing the good instead of the bad. It creates an attention and energy shift toward optimism rather than pessimism.

This research got us to thinking about creating an awe wall for our own marriage. A few years ago, above a little desk near our kitchen, we installed a ribbon board that makes it easy to place all kinds of things that heighten our awareness and amazement. It's proved to be a great investment in our relationship. The board is continually changing. At the moment it displays a little self-portrait sketch by our fifteen-year-old son on a skateboard, a birth announcement for Maddex Farmer (the sweet new baby of dear friends), ticket stubs from a recent comedy show we attended, a photo of the two of us walking at Greenlake (one of our favorite places), a picture of Javier (a little boy we sponsor in El Salvador), a fancy calling card from a coffee roaster at Cannon Beach that brings back great memories . . . You get the idea. Our awe wall is filled with dozens of keepsakes that we love to ponder. It sparks countless conversations and it's always evolving as either one of us contributes to it.

So if pessimism sometimes gets the best of your attempts to celebrate, take the advice of Karen Reivich and her fellow researchers and start an awe wall for your relationship.

Don't Neglect the Celebration of Sex

Comedian Ray Romano, who has four kids, including twins, says his comedy is inspired by real life. "After kids, everything changes," he told *Newsweek*. "We're having sex about every three months. If I have sex, I know my quarterly estimated taxes must be due. And if it's oral sex, I know it's time to renew my driver's license."

Comedians love to poke fun at married sex. Perhaps with good reason. Ever heard of DINS? It stands for Dual-Income, No Sex. Faced with the frantic pace of modern life, the libidos of dual-income couples can get lost in the shuffle. Psychologists estimate that 15 to 20 percent of couples have sex no more than ten times a year, which is how the experts define sexless marriage. A *USA Today* article reports that a whopping forty million married couples have little or no sexual contact with their spouses. And *Time* magazine recently observed, "Sleep is the new sex."[8]

Don't let it be so in your marriage. When it comes to celebrating each other, sex is one of the greatest activities a couple can participate in. After all, it's no secret that a roll in the hay, and all that leads up to it, feels good. Endorphins are the neurotransmitters in your brain that reduce pain and, in the absence of pain, can induce euphoria. A rush of such chemicals might seem like a temporary solution to a dreary day, but there are added benefits, not the least of which is expressing affection and strengthening the bonds of your marriage. Oxytocin is released by the pituitary gland upon orgasm. Often referred to as the *hormone of love* or the *cuddle chemical*, it is associated with feelings of bonding and trust and can even reduce stress.

> Love looks not with the eyes, but with the mind.
>
> *William Shakespeare*

So does sex make couples happy? No doubt about it. In a study, married men and women who reported above-average sexual

> Affection is responsible for nine-tenths of whatever solid and durable happiness there is in our lives.
>
> *C. S. Lewis*

satisfaction in their marriage were ten to thirteen times more likely to describe their marriage as "very happy," compared with those who reported below average sexual satisfaction.[9]

More important than the quantity of sex within marriage is the quality of it. The best sexual encounters are about more than biological release. Sex becomes more deeply pleasurable when it is embedded within the additional pleasure of intense closeness. It's what Isabel Allende was getting at when she said: "For women the best aphrodisiacs are words. The G-spot is in the ears. He who looks for it below there is wasting his time." Emotional intimacy that accompanies sexual intimacy puts sexual satisfaction into the upper echelons of happiness.

We have a friend, sex therapist Dr. Douglas Rosenau, who literally wrote the book on this: *A Celebration of Sex*.[10] He recently told us: "I urge my patient not to be spontaneous about sex. It's overrated and over idealized." What he means is that sexual spontaneity is more fantasy than fact. It may be Hollywood's favorite form of sexual encounter, but it's not the norm for married couples who enjoy a healthy sex life. Why? Because they are *intentional* about sex. And to think that the best sex is always spontaneous is simply not true. In fact, it's a myth. So don't be afraid to plan a celebration of sex into your calendar.

Listen to the Music

According to the *Guinness Book of World Records*, "Happy Birthday To You" is the most recognized song in the English language and has been translated countless times. You'll hear it sung everywhere from San Diego to Kennebunkport; from Shanghai to Abu Dhabi. It was composed in the 1920s and has become a staple at birthday celebrations around the world.

Music, even the simplest of tunes, can touch the human heart and evoke positive emotions like few other experiences.[11] "Without music," said philosopher Friedrich Nietzsche, "life would be a mistake." And it would certainly be a mistake to overlook music as a powerful happiness booster for couples.[12]

When jazz legend John Coltrane first heard Charlie Parker play the saxophone, the music hit him "right between the eyes," he once said. According to neuroscientists, Coltrane was exactly right. When we hear music that we like, even for the first time, a part of the brain's reward system is activated, research shows.[13]

A favorite song, whether a power rock anthem or a soulful acoustic ballad, evokes a deep emotional response. Neuroscientist Valorie Salimpoor recalls once listening to Johannes Brahms's "Hungarian Dance No. 5" while driving. The music moved her so profoundly that she had to pull over. Intrigued by the experience, Salimpoor joined Robert Zatorre at McGill University in Canada to study how music affects the brain. She and Zatorre confirmed that dopamine, a reward neurotransmitter, is the source of such intense experiences—the "chills"—associated with a favorite piece of music.

Music activates parts of the brain that trigger happiness, releasing endorphins similar to the ways that sex and food do. A song we like, be it classical, folk, or punk, causes our brain to fire off with delight. A mini celebration ensues. So what can you do to bring more of these musical celebrations into your relationship?

We have a suggestion. If you're of a certain age, you probably made your partner a playlist when you were dating, a personalized compilation of songs that spoke to the two of you. They may have been songs that conjured certain memories or songs that simply conveyed a message you wanted your partner to hear from you. And if you didn't make a playlist you may have even called into a local radio station to have a particular song dedicated to your sweetheart. Pretty juvenile, right? Well, you didn't used to think so. You spent hours listening to those songs together and apart. Why not put a little playlist together for just the two of you again. It may sound silly, but we dare you.

And if you're wondering, yes, we've done this ourselves—twenty-eight years into our marriage. A little James Taylor singing "Secret O' Life," Al Green's "Let's Stay Together," Dan Fogelberg's "Stolen Moments," and Paul McCartney singing "My Love." We mostly go old school because the songs on our playlist can bring us right back to specific moments in time, early in our relationship, and they conjure fantastic emotions.

Hearing a piece of music is often tied to memories: if this is the song that was playing during a first kiss, then the prefrontal cortex, where memory is stored, lights up. Since this is one of the last brain areas to fall prey to the ravages of Alzheimer's disease, researchers have found that people with the condition can remember songs from long ago, even when they can't remember what they did yesterday.[14]

The gift of music runs deep. Even the most cynical among us would have a hard time denying that hearing a favorite song can completely change our mood. That's why it's essential to bring music into the arena of celebrating each other. As Shakespeare said, "If music be the food of love, play on."

Be Generous in Spirit

We were sitting in an airport terminal recently and observed an older couple seated across from us waiting to board the same plane. She leaned over and asked him a question, looking directly into his eyes. We didn't hear what either of them said, but he smiled and patted her on the knee. A minute later, she got up and brought him a cup of coffee. He looked surprised and delighted.

It wasn't dramatic. In fact, it was barely perceptible. But this couple showed a series of small acts of emotional generosity within a few minutes. And those small acts are what one researcher calls "the best marital life insurance policy there is."[15]

> A kiss is a lovely trick, designed by nature, to stop words when speech becomes superfluous.
>
> *Ingrid Bergmen*

Researchers from the University of Virginia's National Marriage Project recently studied the role of generosity in nearly three thousand marriages. Generosity was defined as "the virtue of giving good things to one's spouse freely and abundantly," like simply making them coffee in the morning or offering a little backrub—things that have little to do with spending money. Researchers quizzed men and women on how often they behaved generously toward their partners.

The responses went right to the core of their unions. Men and women with the highest scores on the generosity scale were far more likely to report that they were "very happy" in their marriages. The benefits of generosity were particularly pronounced among couples with children. Among the parents who posted above-average scores for marital generosity, about 50 percent reported being "very happy" together. Among those with lower generosity scores, only about 14 percent claimed to be "very happy."

"In marriage we are expected to do our fair share when it comes to housework, child care and being faithful, but generosity is going above and beyond the ordinary expectations with small acts of service and making an extra effort to be affectionate," explained Brad Wilcox, who led the research.[16]

Think about that: couples who reported a high amount of generosity in their relationship were five times more likely to say their marriage was "very happy," compared with those who reported a low amount of generosity.

So how do you cultivate a generous spirit in your marriage? You begin by putting away the measuring scales or the scoreboard. If you're keeping track of who gets what ("He went golfing so I'm buying new shoes") you'll never get there. As Saint Thérèse de Lisieux is said to have observed, "When one loves, one does not calculate."

Second, you've got to focus on what your spouse likes. If you know it would mean a lot to your partner to gas up the car or turn down the bed or sweep the porch or watch a particular movie or play a video game together, then that's where you want to put your energy. If your spouse delights in a triple-tall nonfat latte and you get her an almond mocha instead, you've missed the mark. Generosity works best when it signals to your spouse that you know them and their personal desires.

Third, don't neglect the intangibles. Sometimes a spirit of generosity is found when we give our spouse the benefit of the doubt by not questioning their reasoning. It's also found when we give our spouse credit for a good idea. And it's certainly found when we give our time. A generous spirit simply sets selfishness aside and gives.

Finally, if you want to have a generous spirit in your relationship, give without expecting anything in return. This is crucial. Generosity is never a down payment on a gift you're wanting. Generosity is only as valid as the motivation behind it. It must come from the heart with no strings attached. To paraphrase Bob Hope, if your generosity does not come from your heart, you have the worst kind of heart trouble.

A Final Thought on Celebrating Each Other

Sue Johnston, sixty-eight, from Houston, Texas, wrote to a magazine and explained an unexpected surprise she received ten months after she lost her husband, John. Beginning with their first Valentine's day together, John had always sent Sue a beautiful bouquet of flowers containing a note with five simple words: "My love for you grows."

"Four children, 56 bouquets and a lifetime of love were his legacy to me, when he passed away," Sue writes. "On my first Valentine's Day alone, 10 months after I lost him, I was shocked to receive a gorgeous bouquet addressed to me." The flower arrangement was from John. Sue was angry and heartbroken. She called the florist to say there had been a mistake.

The florist replied, "No, ma'am, it's not a mistake. Before he passed away, your husband prepaid for many years and asked us to guarantee that you'd continue getting bouquets every Valentine's Day." Sue's heart was in her throat. She hung up the phone and read the attached card. It said, "My love for you is eternal."

We don't know John, but one thing is certain: he knew how to celebrate Sue. And their story inspires us to celebrate each other—here and now. We pray the same is true for you.

For Reflection

1. What do you think of the statement, "It takes an average of two years to adapt to the newness of marriage. After that, we start to take each other and the relationship for granted." In what ways might you be taking your relationship for granted?

2. When do you feel most celebrated by your partner and why? When do they feel most celebrated by you?

3. Of the half dozen tips for celebrating each other more in this chapter, which ones are you most and least inclined to try and why? When, where, and how—specifically—are you going to try one of the tips?

7 Attune Your Spirits

There is a kind of happiness and wonder that
makes you serious. It is too good to waste on jokes.

C. S. Lewis

IN A SEINFELD EPISODE entitled "The Engagement," Jerry and his
friend George Costanza have decided it's time to "grow up" and treat
the women they date with a little more respect (George has just
broken up with a woman because she beat him in chess).[1] The conversation leaves such an indelible mark on George that he immediately looks up an old girlfriend, goes to her apartment, and asks her
to marry him. Jerry opts for something less extreme: he goes home
and decides to talk about the matter further with his friend Kramer.

Jerry is in his apartment. Kramer stands beside him. Jerry turns
to Kramer and says, "I had a very interesting lunch with George
Costanza today."

"Really?" Kramer responds.

"We were talking about our lives, and we both kind of realized
we're kids—we're not men."

Kramer leans in and says, "So then you asked yourselves, 'Isn't
there something more to life?'"

"Yes, " Jerry says. "Yes, we did!"

"Yeah, well, let me clue you in on something, " Kramer says. "There isn't."

"There isn't?" Jerry replies with a concerned look on his face.

"Absolutely not!" says Kramer. "I mean, what were you thinking about, Jerry? Marriage? Family?"

"Well—"

"They're prisons! Manmade prisons!" Kramer continues. "You're doing time. You get up in the morning. She's there. You go to sleep at night. She's there. It's like you gotta ask permission to use the bathroom." He mocks the imaginary wife, saying with a sneer: "Is it all right if I use the bathroom now?"

"Really?" Jerry says.

"Yeah, and you can forget about watching TV while you're eating," Kramer says.

"I can?"

"Oh, yeah. You know why? Because it's dinner time! And do you know what you do at dinner?"

"What?" Jerry asks.

"You talk about your day! 'How was your day today? Did you have a good day or a bad day today? Well, what kind of day was it? I don't know. How about you? How was your day?'"

"Boy," says Jerry, horrified at the picture that's been painted.

"It's sad, Jerry. It's a sad state of affairs!"

"I'm glad we had this talk," Jerry says to Kramer.

"Oh, you have no idea!" Kramer says.

Actually, Kramer has no idea. The dreary picture he paints of marriage is dead wrong. The happiest people on the planet are married couples who not only debrief their day with each other but also have deep and meaningful conversations to boot. Happy couples are each other's best friends.[2] For good reason too. Marriage affords a kind of emotional intimacy unlike any other relationship. And intimacy, that soul-to-soul connection, is one of the most powerful happiness boosters available.

Defining Intimacy

Robert Sternberg of Yale University studied romantic love long before it was fashionable among scholars. In his groundbreaking project he discovered love's essential ingredients: passion, commitment, and intimacy.[3] Passion is physical. Commitment is willful. And intimacy is emotional. Intimacy is a feeling that says something along the lines of: "You get me and I get you like nobody on the planet." It's the feeling of being deeply in sync with the person you love. It's a feeling of being best friends.[4]

> A happy marriage is a long conversation which always seems too short.
>
> *Andre Maurois*

Look up *intimacy* in a dictionary and you'll see words like *close, warm, familiar, affectionate, caring,* and *understanding.* Some researchers say that intimacy emerges when you see less "me" and "you" in the relationship and more "we" and "us."[5] It engenders interdependence, a detailed knowledge of each other, and a deep sense of belonging.[6]

Intimacy involves two criteria, according to a landmark study.[7] First, intimate partners *share information.* They have secrets. They disclose their plans and provide personal details that they don't share with others. Second, intimate partners not only share information, they have a *deep understanding of each other.* This allows them to know each other's thoughts, habits, and preferences. Mrs. Albert Einstein was once asked if she understood her husband's theory of relativity. "No," she said, "but I know how he likes his tea." That's part of emotional intimacy.

At a meeting for marriage and family therapists some time ago, we heard a speaker define *intimacy* this way: "In-to-me-see." And perhaps that defines the friendship factor of marriage best. Intimacy is seeing into each other's lives. It's being aware of each other's deepest self. This gets to the soul-to-soul connection. It's attuning our spirits. Dr. Don Harvey, in *The Spiritually Intimate Marriage*, said it's being able to share your spiritual self, find this reciprocated, and have a sense of union. Spiritual intimacy causes a couple's spirits to sprout new wings. Deep and abiding spiritual intimacy empowers a couple's relationship to soar.

> There's nothing more intimate in life than simply being understood. And understanding someone else.
>
> *Brad Meltzer*

Intimacy and Happiness

"Woe to him who is alone when he falls and has not another to lift him up," warns the sage of Ecclesiastes. So true. We need the care that comes from intimacy. Without it, we are sure to be unhappy.

The National Opinion Research Center asked people a simple question: "Looking over the last six months, who are the people with whom you discussed matters important to you?" Compared to those who could name no such intimate, those who could immediately name someone were 60 percent more likely to feel "very happy." [8]

Six massive investigations, each interviewing thousands of people across several years, have all reached a common conclusion: intimacy not only increases happiness, it is essential to sustaining it.[9] Those who feel known and understood by family, friends, or a close-knit religious community are not only less vulnerable to stress and disease, their well-being skyrockets. "Intimate attachments to other human beings," wrote psychiatrist John Bowlby, "are the hub around which a person's life revolves."[10] Feeling close to others with whom we can share intimate thoughts and feelings has two effects, observed the seventeenth-century philosopher Francis Bacon: "It redoubleth joys, and cutteth griefs in half." No doubt about it, intimacy and well-being are inextricably linked.

Innumerable medical studies have shown the value of emotional intimacy on recovery, healing, and immunity—not to mention living longer. Intimacy, however, is not only good for the body but great for the soul.[11] And a growing body of research reveals that people with a personal faith cope more effectively and suffer less depression than those who don't.[12] Not only that, believers who incorporate religion into daily living (attending services, reading Scripture, praying), rate higher on two measures of happiness: frequency of positive emotions and overall sense of satisfaction with life.[13]

> There are few stronger predictors of happiness than a close, nurturing, equitable, intimate, lifelong companionship with one's best friend.
>
> *David Myers*

Why study spirituality in connection to intimacy? Because intimacy wades into the shallow waters of life until spirituality brings it to the deep end. When we reveal our soul to another person—or to God—we are getting to the deep core of intimacy. And stacks upon stacks of research reveal that the more spiritually intimate we feel, the happier we are as well.[14]

What Intimacy
Does for Your Relationship

Perhaps the lamest excuse we ever hear for a couple getting a divorce is, "We just seemed to drift apart." Excuse us, but there is no drifting. It is a series of decisions, choices, and attitudes that distance a couple. Fundamentally, it is choices that keep their spirits from connecting. It is decisions that that block intimacy. They quit being friends. "It is not a lack of love," said Friedrich Nietzsche, "but a lack of friendship that makes unhappy marriages." Incidentally, the social scientific evidence clearly shows that the vast majority of divorces occur in relatively low-conflict marriages.[15] A malaise in marriage sets in. And that's due to a lack of emotional intimacy.

> Most beds aren't as intimate as people think they are.
>
> *Malcom Bradbury*

It turns out that after reviewing hundreds of research studies on the various factors that predict stable, happy marriages, scientists are converging on an unexpected primary factor: friendship. In fact, emotional intimacy of friendship trumps romance.[16] Get this: Gallup's research indicates that a couple's friendship quality could account for 70 percent of overall marital satisfaction. In fact, the emotional intimacy that a married couple shares is said to be five times more important than their physical intimacy. That's an incredibly strong indicator of just how important emotional intimacy is to marital happiness.

Premier marriage scholar John Gottman summarizes more than two decades of research and dozens of studies in stating that "the simple truth [is] that happy marriages are based on a deep friendship."[17] Gottman believes that in good marriages, couples achieve an intimate familiarity with each other's quirks, desires, fears, aspirations, and habits. They express this knowledge in big and little ways: "When she orders him a salad, she knows to ask for the dressing on the side. If she works late, he'll tape her favorite TV show because he knows which one it is and when it's on." He calls it a couple's *love map*. And the more you study it, the more intimate you become with all of its details.[18]

> Among men, sex sometimes results in intimacy. Among women, intimacy sometimes results in sex.
>
> *Barbara Cartland*

Make no mistake about it: emotional intimacy in marriage is one of the single most important wellsprings of happiness a couple can ever find.

What's Your Intimacy Quotient?

How well do you know each other? To find out, each of you can take the following questionnaire separately. The more honest you are with your answers, the more insightful will be your results.

Yes   No   I know what stresses my partner currently faces.

Yes   No   I know the names of people who have been irritating my spouse lately.

Yes   No   I know some of my partner's life dreams.

Yes   No   I am very familiar with my partner's religious faith and spiritual quest.

Yes   No   I can outline my partner's basic philosophy of life.

Yes   No   I know my partner's favorite music.

Yes   No   I can list my partner's favorite two or three movies.

Yes   No   I know the most stressful thing that happened to my partner in childhood.

Yes   No   I can list my partner's major aspirations.

Yes   No   I know what my partner would do if he/she won a million dollars.

Yes   No   We regularly attend church together.

Yes   No   I have at least ten minutes of quality conversation with my partner every day.

Yes   No   I feel my partner knows me well.

Yes   No   It's not unusual for my partner and me to pray together.

Yes   No   I feel emotionally intimate with my spouse on most days.

If you answered yes to more than ten of the items, your emotional intimacy with your spouse is likely to be in pretty good shape. The two of you feel pretty in sync. Congratulations! If you had fewer than ten you have room for improvement and you'll find several helps in this chapter to help you do just that.

How to Attune Your Spirits

Good friends are hard to find. And when found—particularly in marriage—we sometimes take them for granted. That's why a bit of intentionality can go a long way in guarding your relationship against the proverbial drift and supercharging your happiness. Each of the tips below is backed up by research. They work. But, as always, lean into the ones that you think will work best for you and your relationship.

Prime the Pump for Great Conversations

If we were meeting across the table from each other right now, instead of through the pages of this book, we'd ask your permission to talk one on one, Les with the husband and Leslie with the wife. Since we can't do that, we divide this tip into two sections.

Especially for men: if your wife were to rate how romantic you've been in the last three months, what would she say? Are you cringing? A survey of more than fifteen hundred married women revealed that they are starving for romance.[19] And with good reason. A full 45 percent of women say they have not been offered a coat when cold and 53 percent have never been whisked away for an exciting surprise. Why?

It's not laziness. Research reveals that we men severely underestimate the romantic value of even the simplest act. We can do better. Here's a little list created by married women that might help:

- Cover her eyes and lead her to a lovely surprise.
- Tell her she is the most wonderful woman you've ever met.
- Run her a relaxing bath.
- Leave a romantic note around the house for her to find.
- Offer her a coat when she is cold.

Note, by the way, that none of these ideas involve spending a single dime. Blatant acts of materialism trail in last place on lists of romantic acts for most women. It really is the thought that counts.

Especially for women: When was the last time you gave your husband a proverbial gold star? That is, when have you last affirmed him? Predictably, studies show that receiving a spouse's affirmation (expressions of appreciation, desire, or support) is very important to both husbands and wives. But they are more important to husbands. Why? They depend on us for reassurance and understanding because they typically don't find it in their friendships like we do. If they want praise or sympathy or the chance to talk over a sensitive subject, it's you that your husband is looking to.

Here's the bottom line: research shows that partners who make thoughtful efforts for each other are far more likely to open up in conversation than those who don't. Shocker, right? But every time we give our spouse the emotional gifts they need, we are priming the pump for more intimate and positive conversations.

Reclaim the Ten Minutes You May Have Been Missing

Early on in our marriage we seemed to talk about everything. Nothing was off limits. We talked at length about our dreams, our struggles, our fears, and our triumphs. In short we were vulnerable. We shared things we didn't dare share with anyone else. But somewhere along the line (certainly after our children were born) these heart-to-heart chitchats dwindled—along with the intimacy they engendered. We were still talking, of course, but not the kind of vulnerable talks we once shared.

"You can have a two-hour conversation and not talk about anything of substance or value or quality," said Terri Orbuch at the Institute for Social Research at the University of Michigan. She and her colleagues studied 373 married couples for more than twenty years and came up with a prescription for increasing emotional intimacy: ten minutes a day for quality conversation. "Many couples think they're communicating with each other when they sort out who will pick up the kids, pay the bills, or call the grandparents," said Orbuch. But that's not the kind of communication she's talking about. Her research and many others consistently show a link between happy marriages and "self-disclosure," or sharing your private feelings, fears, doubts, and perceptions with your partner.

> Intimacy is the capacity to be rather weird with someone—and finding that that's ok with them.
>
> *Alain De Botton*

Why is this important? Because the early stages of marriage, research shows, characterized by open and frequent conversations, typically declines if couples are not intentional—especially when kids come along. In other words, as your marriage matures, self-disclosure

> Communication leads
> to community, that is, to
> understanding, intimacy and
> mutual valuing.
>
> *Rollo May*

risks leveling off.[20] Don't let it happen. Too much is at stake. Try Dr. Orbuch's advice. We did. Rarely does a day go by that we don't have at least ten minutes of vulnerable talk time. It's typically after our boys are tucked in and the house is quiet. Occasionally it's over lunch together, depending on our schedules. What do we talk about? We focus on the 5 percent of our life we generally don't discuss with others. Try it. Reclaim the heart-to-heart connections you may be missing. You're sure to see your emotional intimacy levels increase.

List Your Spouse's Top Ten Faults—Not

A grandmother, celebrating her golden wedding anniversary, once told the secret of her long and happy marriage. "On my wedding day, I decided to make a list of ten of my husband's faults which, for the sake of our marriage, I would overlook," she said.

A guest asked the woman what some of the faults she had chosen to overlook were. The grandmother replied, "To tell you the truth, my dear, I never did get around to listing them. But whenever my husband did something that made me hopping mad, I would say to myself, *Lucky for him that's one of the ten!*"

Couples who are able to acknowledge their partner's faults while maintaining positive views of their marriage overall experience more happiness and have more stable satisfaction over time.[21] It makes sense. After all, we can't simply ignore the things that drive us nuts. I, Les, for example, after more than twenty-five years of marriage with Leslie, still find it incredulous that she doesn't live life with a little more organization. Whether it's managing money or simply knowing what we need to buy at the market, Leslie is a free spirit. It drives me nuts—but it's also one of the things I love about her. She's the disorganized *yin* to my uptight *yang*.

It took us the better part of our first decade to appreciate each other's faults. And we're still working on it. But here's what we've learned: when you surrender your need to change your partner's "faults," you also let go of the need to be irritated by them. You begin to accept them as part of who your partner is—and you actually have a chance to let those quirks become the things that endear you to him or her. The negatives become positives.

That's what researchers mean by managing a positive view of your marriage while acknowledging faults. If you can accept the faults without letting them drag you into negativity, you strengthen your relationship and up the ante for more emotional intimacy.

Pray It Forward

Couples that pray together . . . You know the rest. But it's more than a catchy saying. A University of Chicago survey of married couples found that 75 percent of Americans who pray with their spouses reported their marriages are "very happy" (compared to 57 percent of those who don't). Those who pray together are also more likely to say they respect each other, discuss their marriage together, and—stop the presses—rate their spouses as skilled lovers.[22]

Whether it's a simple grace at dinnertime or some soul-searching meditation, couples routinely say that a shared spiritual life helps keep them close and stokes the fires of emotional intimacy.

"We have been married for nine years, but praying together is something we didn't start doing until about a year ago," says our friend Daniel, a thirty-eight-year-old biochemist in Seattle. "In the past, whenever we faced big decisions, we'd have discussion after discussion about them, but we'd never really come to a resolution. Prayer began to change that for us." Jacquie, his wife, agrees: "When we pray, it brings another level of honesty to our conversations. I think it's the most intimate thing you can do with another person."

Like Daniel and Jacquie, 32 percent of American married couples pray together regularly.[23] Some hold hands. Some pray quietly or silently. Others pray out loud. Some pray before dinner. Some in bed. Some ask for forgiveness or give thanks. Whatever the time, place, or style, prayer is a powerful source of intimacy.

But here's a prayer secret most couples don't know: couples who practice meditative prayer are happier overall and feel closer to God than those who practice other kinds of payer, such as petitioning for relief or asking for blessings.[24] Meditative prayer occurs when we simply practice being "in the presence" of God. Brother Lawrence, the Parisian lay brother who worked most of his life in the kitchen of a monastery, literally wrote the book on it. "How happy we would be if we could find the treasure of which the Gospel speaks," he said. "Let us search unceasingly and let us not stop until we have found it." That treasure? To be in relationship with God, of course.

> The soul must always stand ajar, ready to welcome the ecstatic experience.
>
> *Emily Dickinson*

So if you don't do so already, consider praying it forward in your relationship. Pray for each other. Pray for your family. Give thanks for your blessing. But don't neglect prayer that simply seeks to have a relationship with God. When you walk together with God, intimacy will find you.

Get Your Church On

British theologian and acclaimed author C. S. Lewis described happiness fifty years ago in terms that make even more sense today in our fast-paced society:

A car is made to run on [gasoline], and it would not run properly on anything else. Now God designed the human machine to run on himself. He himself is the fuel our spirits were designed to burn, or the food our spirits were designed to feed on. There is no other. That is why it is just no good asking God to make us happy in our own way without bothering about religion. God cannot give us a happiness and peace apart from himself, because it is not there. There is no such thing.[25]

> Happiness of heart can no more be attained without God than light and sunshine can be had without the sun.
>
> *Bernard Vaughan*

Researchers seem to agree. Survey after survey shows that people with strong religious faith—those who are relating to God—are happier than those who are irreligious.[26] David Myers, a social psychologist at Michigan's Hope College, said that faith provides social support, a sense of purpose, and a reason to focus beyond the self, all of which help root people and lead to greater connection and happiness. And the most concrete expression of our faith is often attending church.

According to sociologist W. Bradford Wilcox of the University of Virginia, married couples who attend church together tend to be happier than couples who rarely or never attend services.[27] Wilcox found that married church-going Americans across denominational and racial classifications were more likely to describe themselves as "very happy" than their nonreligious counterparts. "Attending church only seems to help couples when they attend together," said Wilcox. And he was quick to add that it's not simply attending church that works some kind of magic. "You've got to combine faith and works to enjoy a happy and stable marriage. You need the consistent message, the accountability, and the support a church community can provide to really benefit from religious faith."[28]

The two of us have been going to church our entire lives. Literally. We both grew up in the homes of ministers. We were PK's—preacher's kids. So we've known the benefits of going to church. But because it's such a part of our lives we run the risk of it becoming part of a mundane routine, like putting gas in our car. So a few years ago we decided to be intentional about church in our lives. It starts when we get in our car and turn on our Sunday morning playlist. It includes songs we've long associated with church, songs that are particularly meaningful to us. We also make it a point to hold hands at some point in the service. It's our way of saying we are fully present, not just going through the motions. And we always debrief our worship service over brunch, noting what was particularly helpful or salient. You get the idea. So if going to church has become just another thing you do, try giving it a boost of attention.

A Final Thought on Attuning Your Spirits

As we leave you in this chapter that has been dedicated to helping the two of you cultivate more emotional intimacy, up your friendship factor, and attune your spirits, we want to share the following quotes from two imaginary journal entries as a wife and her husband reflect on the same day's events:

Her Journal

Tonight, my husband was acting weird. We had made plans to meet at a nice restaurant for dinner. Conversation wasn't flowing, so I suggested that we go somewhere quiet so we could talk. He agreed, but he didn't say much. I asked him what was wrong. He said, "Nothing." I asked him if it was my fault that he was upset. He said he wasn't upset, that it had nothing to do with me, and not to worry about it. On the way home, I told him that I loved him. He smiled slightly and kept driving. When we got home, he just sat there quietly and watched TV. He continued to seem distant and absent. Finally, with silence all around us, I decided to go to bed. About fifteen minutes later he came to bed. But I still felt that he was distracted and his thoughts were somewhere else. He fell asleep. I don't know what to do.

His Journal

Rough day. Boat wouldn't start, can't figure out why.

Sure, the words are fictitious, but the emotional experience is as real as it gets. Men and women do not approach deep and meaningful conversation the same way. While we both long for emotional intimacy together, we don't always process it or express it with the same vocabulary. So as you work to attune your spirits together, offer each other grace and understanding.

For Reflection

1. When and where do you feel most emotionally intimate with your spouse and why?
2. It's difficult to exaggerate the importance of cultivating the friendship factor in marriage. Do you see how it is actually choices that determine its vitality and not "drift"? Do you agree?
3. One of the tips in this chapter for increasing intimacy, and thus happiness, is to reclaim the ten minutes of meaningful conversation you may be missing. Are you likely to put this into practice? Why or why not?

8 Add Value to Others

> Unless we think of others and do something for
> them, we miss one of the greatest sources
> of happiness.
>
> *Ray L. Wilbur*

"If you could give just one sentence of marital advice to these two hundred students before you leave, what would it be?" It's the closing question we pose every Monday evening to a guest couple in our Marriage 101 class at Seattle Pacific University. After our evening's lecture we always have a real-life couple come in for a brief interview. And we end every interview with that question. Typically, the husband and wife look at each other as if to say, "You go first." And eventually one of them does. Occasionally we need to remind them it's just one sentence, but always they give our students a pearl of wisdom.

We've been doing this for nearly two decades and even after twenty-eight years of marriage ourselves, we're just as curious as our students to see what these couples say. Here's a sample:

- "If you don't learn how to forgive, you won't learn how to stay married."

- "What is now, will be then, only more so."
- "Don't skimp on your lingerie budget."
- "When you argue—and you will—make sure you know what the fight is about."

Our students write down what our guests say and by the end of the semester they have a treasure trove of marital wisdom. And so do we. You're never too experienced to learn from the experiences of others. "When people tell me they've learned from experience," said Warren Buffet, "I tell them the trick is to learn from other people's experience." We couldn't agree more—especially when it comes to marriage.

Defining Kindness

It was written for the first time on a placemat at a restaurant in Sausalito, California: "Practice random acts of kindness and senseless acts of beauty." When Ann Herbert wrote the phase in the 1980s, she had no idea that it would spread far and wide. The phrase appears on thousands of bumper stickers and plaques, not to mention being featured on an Oprah Winfrey show—all because of what Ann wrote on a placemat.

She succinctly captured what tugs at the heart of every healthy human: selfless actions to assist or cheer up others. Kind acts embody an uncalculating attitude that desires neither monetary payment nor human applause. Some call it benevolence, goodwill, generativity, or altruism. But the word *kindness* seems the most straight forward. It comes from the Saxon word meaning "family" or "kin." That makes sense. When we are kind, even to a stranger, we are treating them like family.

Kindness sets aside our fear of being exploited. It relinquishes self-focus. Kindness causes us to pause from our own pursuits in order to augment somebody else's. In short, acts of kindness add value to others.

How Adding Value to Others
Boosts Your Happiness

World-renowned scholar Bernard Rimland specialized in autism. In fact, he viewed the cure of autism as a quest, a personal calling, writing books on the subject and raising money for research. But Dr. Rimland did a startlingly simple experiment along the way that sheds light on happiness. He asked 216 students to list the initials of ten people they knew best, yielding a grand total of about two thousand people. He then asked the students to note whether each person seemed happy or not. Finally he asked them to review each person again, indicating if the person seemed selfish (devoted mostly to his or her own welfare) or unselfish (willing to be inconvenienced for others).

> The only really happy people are those who have learned how to serve.
>
> *Rick Warren*

The result: 70 percent of those judged unselfish seemed happy. Ninety-five percent of those judged selfish seemed unhappy. What a paradox. "Selfish people are, by definition, those whose activities are devoted to bringing themselves happiness," said Rimland. "Yet, at least as judged by others, these selfish people are far less likely to be happy than those whose efforts are devoted to making others happy."

To be sure, the notion of kindness leading to happiness is not new. Writers, philosophers, and religious thinkers have made the connection for centuries. Scottish-born essayist Thomas Carlyle quipped that "without kindness, there can be no true joy." Mark Twain said, "The best way to cheer yourself is to try to cheer someone else up." Pastor Rick Warren noted, "The only really happy people are those who have learned how to serve." And then there's a saying that goes like this:

If you want to be happy . . .
. . . for an hour, take a nap.
. . . for a day, go fishing.
. . . for a month, get married.
. . . for a year, get an inheritance.
. . . for a lifetime, help others.

But it was only recently that these sentiments were put to the test to see if helping really did increase happiness. Sonja Lyubomirsky and her collaborators at the University of California, Riverside recruited participants and asked them to perform five acts of kindness per week over the course of six weeks.[1] Every Sunday night the participants turned in their "kindness reports" in which they described the acts of kindness they had done, to whom, and when.

As expected, being generous and considerate made people happy. In fact, they experienced a significant elevation in their happiness. But this was only the first of many experiments showing that kindness does indeed cause happiness (not that it merely correlates with it). Since this first study, the research team at UC Riverside has conducted longer and more intensive investigations, all of which underscore how powerful acts of kindness are to increasing happiness.

What Adding Value to Others Does for Your Relationship

Deitrich Bonhoeffer, the German theologian who was hanged by the Nazis during World War II, wrote a wonderful wedding sermon while he was in prison, but he never had a chance to deliver it in person.[2] He said:

> Marriage is more than your love for each other. It has a higher dignity and power, for it is God's holy ordinance . . . In your love you see only the heaven of your happiness, but in marriage you are placed at a post of responsibility toward the world and mankind. Your love is your own private possession, but marriage is something more than personal—it is a status, an office . . . that joins you together in the sight of God.

Have you thought about the "higher dignity and power" of your marriage? Have you thought recently about your marital "post of responsibility" to reach out to the world as a team, the two of you together? Doing good as two married people transcending yourselves to become part of something larger?

Marriage is a great means to doubling your goodwill. It is a great motivator to "spur one another on toward love and good deeds."[3] Two people joined in marriage, as Bonhoeffer said, are ordained to serve others as a team. As a partnership, two people can serve other people better than they could as separate individuals. So don't neglect the increased value of shared service and collaborative acts of kindness. When you do, you are almost always doubly blessed.

What's Your Giving Quotient?

How are you doing as a couple when it comes to adding value to others? Take this little questionnaire to gain a bit of self-reflection and see. Simply answer each question with honesty.

1. Our friends would describe us as being generous of spirit.

   Not at all   *Absolutely*
   1   2   3   4   5   6   7   8   9   10

2. We have done something together for someone in need within the last month.

   Not at all   *Absolutely*
   1   2   3   4   5   6   7   8   9   10

3. We know the experience of satisfaction and joy that comes from doing a project together that improved another's life.

   Not at all   *Absolutely*
   1   2   3   4   5   6   7   8   9   10

4. We have done some specific acts of goodwill together that nobody but the two of us know about.

   Not at all   *Absolutely*
   1   2   3   4   5   6   7   8   9   10

5. We are on the lookout for ways we can encourage and help others.

   Not at all   *Absolutely*
   1   2   3   4   5   6   7   8   9   10

   Total Score: _____

   ### Making Sense of Your Score

   Your score can range anywhere between 5 and 50. The higher your score, the more likely you are to be adding value to others. In other words, the two of you are intentional about doing acts of kindness together. Regardless of your score, however, every couple can move more and more into doing good together.

How to Add Value to Others

"We make a living by what we get," said Winston Churchill. "We make a life by what we give." Regardless of what you do to make a living, the following tips are designed to help you make a life—and a happy marriage—by giving your life away together. Tune into the tips that seem to make the most sense to you.

Make a List of Kind Acts You Can Share

Did you know lists can save lives? It's true. Reporter Atul Gawande made it clear in his *New Yorker* article entitled, "The Checklist."[4] He noted that the average patient in an Intensive Care Unit requires 178 individual actions per day. What if 1 percent of these critical medical adjustments, such as tilting the patients bed thirty degrees, was missed? Would that further illness or death? To find the answer, medical researchers created a checklist for all patients on mechanical ventilation. With a list to go by, the proportion of patients who didn't receive the recommended care dropped from 74 percent to 4 percent.

Lists not only save lives, they spur creativity. The technique is very simple in principle: state your issue or question in the top of a blank sheet of paper and come up with a list of one hundred answers.

> I've told you these things for a purpose: that my joy might be your joy, and your joy wholly mature. This is my command: Love one another the way I loved you.
>
> *John 15:11 (MSG)*

For example, one might use the heading "100 Ways to Improve My Relationships." Yes, 100 may seem like way too many, but apparently it is the exaggeration that makes this list technique work so well.[5]

So here's what we're recommending: together make a list of at least fifty actions you can take to demonstrate a new and special act of kindness beyond your relationship (go for one hundred if you're overachievers). We say "new and special" because you're already doing acts of kindness even if you're not thinking much about it. This list is dedicated to *new* actions.

Now, we've got to be honest. When we did this for the first time it was incredibly difficult. We could easily note things we do on our own, but doing acts of kindness together was a challenge—at first. Once we got started, however, the ideas began to flow more easily. Here's a sample:

- Visit Dave in the hospital.
- Send the Webbers a photo and a thank you for the time they had us to their cabin last summer.
- Give the board books our kids have outgrown to Sarah at church.
- Pick up garbage around Denny Park.
- Give a huge tip to our server at Chinooks.
- Give granola bars to the homeless guy on Virginia Street.
- Call Lucy together and let he know we think of her often.
- Donate together at the local blood bank.
- Thank our postal carrier.
- Smile at the grumpy grocery clerk.
- Give Jake and Crista a night out by babysitting for them.

And so on. The key is specificity. Meaning, instead of writing down "bring flowers to someone," note to whom you'll bring them. And just let the ideas flow. The list does not obligate you. So let it rip.

By the way, in our experience, making this list together raised our mindfulness of shared kindness and we discovered countless spontaneous acts we might have otherwise neglected.

Concentrate Your Kindness When You Can

Remember the study by Sonja Lyubomirsky and her collaborators at UC–Riverside that we noted earlier in this chapter? When she had her subjects perform five acts of kindness per week over the course of six weeks she not only proved that kindness creates happiness, she discovered that when we concentrate our kindness it supercharges our joy.[6]

She divided her participants into two groups. The first group was instructed to do these acts anytime throughout the week. The second

> Happiness is a perfume
> you cannot pour on others
> without getting a few
> drops on yourself.
>
> *Og Mandino*

group was instructed to do the five acts on a single day each week. Would there be a difference in the level of happiness for each group? As expected both groups boosted their happiness levels. But interestingly, this boost was significantly higher for the group that concentrated a lot of their kindness into a single day.

Why would this be? Lyubomirsky believes it's due to being more mindful and intentional. "Many of the kind acts that the participants performed were small ones," she said. "Spreading them over seven days each week might have diminished their conspicuousness, their prominence, and their power or made them less distinguishable from their participants' habitual kind of behavior." The point is that doing more kindness than is your custom is what super charges your happiness.

So try a little experiment of your own together. Review the list of kind acts you made in the previous tip and select five or six that you both feel you could do together in one day. Of course you may want to have some acts that you do separately during the appointed day, but make sure that most of them are acts of kindness you can do together. Then make sure your pillow talk that evening involves reviewing your experience. If you're like most couples, you'll notice a spike in good feelings. So much so that you might want to schedule a day of intentional kindness together on a regular basis.

Try Shared Service in Secret

Dennis and Lucy Gurnsey mentored us early on in our marriage. And one of the many things we learned from them was the value of serving others together. They had the gift of hospitality and they made their home the hub of celebration and delicious dinners for people. Sometimes it was casual and spontaneous, sometimes planned and elegant, but always it was special. They threw graduation parties, birthday parties, and welcome-to-the-neighborhood parties. They had showers and receptions. And every Mother's Day they would have over a dozen single moms over for Sunday brunch.

Needless to say, everyone who knew Dennis and Lucy knew that they shared this gift of serving others through hospitality. But nobody knew about something else they did for others. It was in one of our mentoring sessions when they suggested we try doing some goodwill for someone and not telling them or anyone else about it. In fact, they gave us a challenge. They asked us to dream up something kind that could be done covertly for someone—something that we wouldn't even reveal to Dennis and Lucy.

And we did. We planned a random act of kindness for a person we knew was in need and we didn't tell her or anyone else. Even to this day, well over a decade later, only the two of us know about it. It was our first act of shared service in secret. We call it the *Triple-S*. And we've been honing our service skills on it ever since.

> The most truly generous persons are those who give silently without hope of praise or reward.
>
> *Carol Ryrie Brink*

There's something about doing good for someone when only the two of you know about it that brings your spirits together. Are you willing to take the Triple-S Challenge? Consider how your kindness could go covert. Plan some clandestine goodwill. And keep it as your secret.

Vary Your Kind Acts When Possible

Research makes it clear: helping others on a regular basis makes people happy for an extended period. But here's what you might not know: when you vary what you do to help others it makes an enormous difference in your happiness. In one study, participants who had to repeat their kind acts over and over again actually dropped in happiness by the middle of the study before bouncing back to their original levels. If we don't vary our goodwill it becomes just another item on our to-do list. It becomes tedious and actually detracts rather than adds to happiness. The point is to avoid falling into a rut when practicing kindness. Keep it fresh. Vary what you do.

Close to our home in Seattle is a man, Richard, who stands in the same place most days, just outside of Whole Foods. We see him every week. We've talked to him. We know his sad story of alcoholism and his struggle to avoid homelessness. He's got an upbeat spirit and will sing you a song for a dollar.

We've known Richard for about three years. And we've given him countless dollars over that time. And we've heard his entire repertoire of songs. In fact, we became so accustomed to Richard holding his handmade "Will sing for food" sign that we started scheming for ways to avoid him. It was becoming a drag to know we'd likely need to talk with him unless he was singing for someone else. We even talked about going to another grocery store, even though this one was close to us.

So what did we do? We told Richard that giving him a dollar or two every week wasn't going to happen anymore. We told him we'd give him a more significant gift every so often but that the single-dollar routine was not happening. "Cool," was his reply. "Just let me know when you want a song and it's on the house."

The bottom line is that putting change into a stranger's parking meter or taking out someone's garbage gives you a lift the first few times you do it,

> Let no one ever come to you without leaving better and happier. Be the living expression of God's kindness: kindness in your face, kindness in your eyes, kindness in your smile.
>
> *Mother Teresa*

but after awhile you will adapt to the new habit and it will not longer provide much of an uplift. This doesn't mean, of course, that you should necessarily stop doing it. But it does mean that if it makes sense you might want to mix it up. And, by the way, the research only shows this is true for more minor acts of kindness. It doesn't apply to bigger commitments like fund-raising for a cause, tutoring a student, visiting a sick neighbor, or mentoring another couple.

Consider Marriage Mentoring

We've been teaching relationship courses at the university level for nearly two decades and if there's one thing we know is true about that experience it is this: if you want to learn something, teach it. It's an age-old adage that we're reminded of nearly every time we finish a lecture.

Have you discovered this insight? Once you try to effectively convey principles or skills to someone else, you have to become expert in those principles and skills yourself. For example, if you want to help another couple manage conflict more effectively, you can't help but to improve this aspect of your own relationship.

That's why in 1991 we began linking faculty and staff couples at our university with students who were engaged or newlywed. We called it *marriage mentoring*. It didn't take long until we were running out of mentor couples, so we started recruiting them from area churches. We wrote a little booklet called *The Marriage Mentor Manual* and it wasn't long before we were doing training events for marriage mentoring in churches around the country. Soon we had a video kit called *The Complete Guide to Marriage Mentoring*. More recently we launched the online Marriage Mentoring Academy, making it easier than ever to be trained and certified as a Marriage Mentor couple. To date, we've trained a quarter million couples.

A day doesn't go by in our lives that we don't hear from a marriage mentor couple somewhere. And they inevitably say the same thing: "I think we get more out of this experience than the couple we're mentoring." It's so common we call it the *boomerang effect*. "It never occurred to us that mentoring another couple would make us feel so good," said David and Tammy. "Something about working as a team to help another couple brought us closer ourselves."

> Seek to do good, and you will find that happiness will run after you.
>
> *James Freeman Clarke*

Now you don't have to be a teacher to teach. You don't have to have a PhD or be widely read. If you have a solid marriage and the willingness to allow another couple to learn from your experiences, you are in a prime place to become marriage mentors. What does it involve? A little bit of training and you're off and running to meet couple to couple.

Marriage mentoring applies to every stage and phase of married life. You might be in a position to mentor engaged couples, newlyweds, a couple about to have their first baby, a couple in distress, a couple raising teenagers or about to have an empty nest. Marriage mentors lift up and guide couples at crucial crossroads.

By the way, couples are crying out for this kind of relationship. In a recent survey, 62 percent of respondents said they'd like to find a mentor couple in their church and 92 percent said they would especially like to have a mentor to help them through tough times.

So what about the two of you? Are you ready to explore the idea of becoming marriage mentors? We've made it fun and easy. You can do the training online at your own convenience (with just eight sessions of about twenty minutes each—see www.MarriageMentoring.com).

Marriage mentoring is perhaps the most important and effective way a couple can add value to others. And the boomerang effect of blessing and happiness mentor couples experience is immeasurable.

Consider Sponsoring a Child

Warren Schmidt is leading a life of quiet desperation. He retires from a job at an insurance company, looks back on a meaningless life, and ahead to a meaningless retirement. This sets the stage for the critically acclaimed movie *About Schmidt*, starring Jack Nicholson.

One day, while watching television, Warren sees an opportunity to give money and write letters to an underprivileged child in Tanzania. Warren responds to the appeal, and throughout the movie he faithfully sends the twenty-two dollars a month and writes poignant letters to a child named Ndugu.

On one occasion, after a long road trip, Warren comes home to an empty house. He reluctantly walks in with an armload of impersonal junk mail. He ambles up the stairs and looks disappointedly at the disheveled state of his bedroom. Throughout this scene, the audience hears Warren's voice-over narration of a letter he recently composed to Ndugu. He pours out his intense feeling of emptiness:

> I know we're all pretty small in the scheme of things, and I guess the best you can hope for is to make some kind of difference ... What difference has my life made to anyone? None that I can think of. Hope things are fine with you.
>
> Yours truly, Warren Schmidt

At the end of the narration, the depression on Warren's face gives way to wonder as he stares down at a letter from Tanzania. It is a letter from a nun who works in the orphanage where six-year-old Ndugu lives. She tells Warren that Ndugu thinks of him every day and hopes he is happy. Enclosed is a picture drawn by Ndugu for Warren—two stick people smiling and holding hands. Warren is overcome by the realization that he has finally made a difference.

Implausible? Hardly. Countless people have found deep meaning and joy in sponsoring a needy child. More than five billion dollars per year is channeled into sponsorship programs from ordinary people wanting to make a difference. That equates to nine million children sponsored worldwide.[7] Does it work? Is it effective? Bruce Wydick, professor of economics and international studies at the University of San Francisco, recently conducted independent research in six countries and found unequivocal results: "You could beat this data senseless, and it was incapable of showing anything other than extremely large and statistically significant impacts on educational outcomes for sponsored children." Overall, sponsorship makes children 27 to

40 percent more likely to complete secondary school, and 50 to 80 percent more likely to complete a university education. There's even a positive spillover effect on the unsponsored younger siblings of sponsored children.

We wouldn't be suggesting that you consider sponsoring a needy child if we didn't do so ourselves. In fact, we started sponsoring kids very early on. Currently we have a special interest in a little guy named Javier in Honduras. Like Schmidt, we communicate by mail and love receiving his pictures.

> Happiness doesn't result from what we get, but from what we give.
>
> *Ben Carson*

If you think this is something the two of you would be interested in, you can learn more about World Vision on its Web site (http://www.lesandleslie.com/worldvision/).

A Final Thought on Adding Value to Others

There is an ancient tale about a young girl walking through a meadow when she saw a butterfly impaled on a thorn. Artfully she released the butterfly, which started to fly away. Then it came back, changed into a beautiful fairy. "For your kindness," she told the little girl, "I will grant your fondest wish." The little girl thought for a moment and replied, "I want to be happy." The fairy leaned toward her and whispered in her ear and then suddenly vanished.

As the girl grew, no one in the land was happier than she. Whenever anyone asked her for the secret of her happiness, she would only smile and say, "I listened to a good fairy."

As she grew old, the neighbors were afraid the fabulous secret might die with her. "Tell us, please," they begged. "Tell us what the fairy said." The lovely old lady simply smiled and said, "She told me that everyone, no matter how secure they seem, has need of me!"

It's true. When we embrace the fact that we can be helpful to everyone—especially to the love of our life—life gets easier. Of course, some will argue that this is not the secret to happiness but to misery. These people have never experienced the joy of being needed.

Now if you're not inclined to hear this message from an ancient fairy-tale, take it from science. Dr. Hans Selye, a renowned endocrinologist, stood on a mountain of research when he proclaimed that the happiest people win the gratitude of people around them. Selye rephrased the biblical quote, "Love thy neighbor as thyself," into his own personal code: "Earn thy neighbor's love." Rather than trying to accumulate more money or power, he suggested we acquire goodwill by helping others. "Hoard goodwill," Dr. Selye advised, "and your house will be a storehouse of happiness."

For Reflection

1. What was the last thing the two of you did together to add value to others? Be as specific as you can. What did it do for your relationship?

2. Of all the tips in this chapter for helping you as a couple to add value to others, which one are you most inclined to try and which one are you least inclined to try? Why?

3. Are you inclined to explore the idea of becoming trained to mentor other couples? Why or why not?

PART THREE

C'mon, Get Happy!

9 Overcoming the Biggest Hurdles to Happiness As a Couple

When one door of happiness closes, another opens. But often we look so long at the closed door that we do not see the one which has been opened for us.

Helen Keller

THE POLICE DEPARTMENT OF Dallas, Texas, recently joined a growing number of agencies getting rid of complicated codes used in radio calls or signals. Instead, operators and officers now communicate through a plain-language system that relies on ordinary words and phrases.

For example, in the past an officer might have radioed in to say, "I'm approaching a Code 7 on Highland Ave." Now they just say, "I'm approaching a minor accident on Highland."

The switch is due in large part to the terrorist attacks of September 11, 2001. During the chaos that resulted from the attacks, many federal agencies and officers had trouble communicating with each other because they used different codes for different situations—or worse, similar codes that had different meanings between agencies. As a result of that confusion, federal officials mandated that plain language be used when police and other federal agents respond to major disasters. Many local police and fire departments have followed suit.

"It's just common sense," said Herb Ebsen, a senior corporal with the Dallas Police Department. "If we start speaking in codes, you have a real chance for a problem or misinterpretation."[1]

In much the same way, we've attempted to decode happiness in this book. We've done our best in the previous chapters to uncover the most effective boosters to your happiness as a couple. But in the final section of this book we feel compelled to expose what causes too many couples to miss out on their share of happiness together.

To be clear, we're not saying you can or should *always* be happy. That's not even a worthy goal. As Solomon wrote long ago: "[There's] a time to weep and a time to laugh, a time to mourn and a time to dance."[2] But research reveals that when it is time to laugh and dance—to be happy—many of us aren't. Why?

> People are just as happy as they make up their minds to be.
>
> *Abraham Lincoln*

For starters, because we humans hold fast to a number of wrong ideas about what will make us happy. For example, as we saw in Part One, we think more money will make us happy. It doesn't. To turn a phrase from the New Testament, "The love of money is the root of an unhappy marriage." Research reveals that couples who hang their happiness on finances often have miserable marriages. After interviewing over seventeen hundred couples, a study concluded that "those who draw a lot of happiness from money and possessions do not make for happy spouses." Discontentment and ingratitude around money linked to "less effective communication, higher levels of negative conflict, lower relationship satisfaction, and less marriage stability."[3] Materialism and matrimony don't make good bedfellows.

But the biggest reason we don't find abiding happiness or joy is because we are pursuing happiness for its own sake. Remember the *hedonistic paradox* from our first chapter? When one aims solely towards pleasure itself, one's aim is continually frustrated. It's what Aldous Huxley was getting at when he said: "Happiness is not achieved by the conscious pursuit of happiness; it is generally the by-product of other activities." And it's what Ashley Montagu meant when he said, "The moments of happiness we enjoy take us by surprise. It is not that we seize them, but that they seize us."

No doubt about it: pursuing a feel-good lifestyle at the expense of a values-based life is the road to ruin. Perusing happiness alone can be a fool's errand. But assuming you avoid this emotional misadventure, you're still not necessarily in the clear. You're bound to encounter a few hazards. So in this chapter we're going to say it straight. We are going to expose the hurdles that can steal your happiness if you let them.

The Hazards of Making Happy

Every golfer knows that the greatest golf courses in the world are artfully designed with bunkers and hazards that make each hole more challenging, more interesting. That's why a skilled golfer surveys the course and makes note of where he's likely to have trouble, paying special attention to the hazards.

The same is true for all of us. We do better in life and marriage when we survey our journey ahead and make note of the potential hazards to our happiness. Here are five to keep an eye on.

Comparing Ourselves to Others

"Did you see Rick and Sandy's fancy new car?" "Did you see Dan and Angela's vacation photos on Facebook?" "Did you hear about the poem Ryan wrote his wife on their anniversary?"

Simple questions like these are all it takes to trigger the hazard of social comparison. And it's so tempting, isn't it? We compulsively compare how we're doing to those around us. And inevitably some people do better than we do. What then? If we're like most people, we feel dissatisfied, discontent, or unhappy.

Researchers call it *envy spiral*. It's what happens when we unfavorably compare ourselves with our peers. And they're finding that Facebook is a major contributor. The University of Edinburgh Business School published a report saying that the more social circles you have on Facebook, the more stressed out you're likely to be. The study concluded, "Indeed, access to copious positive news and the profiles of seemingly successful 'friends' fosters social comparison that can readily provoke envy and discontent."[4]

A *Time* magazine poll found that 60 percent of respondents said they do not feel better about themselves after spending time on social media and 76 percent believe other people make themselves look happier on their Facebook page than they really are. Another study found that the more a purchase was motivated by an effort to impress other people, the less of a happiness boost it conferred.[5]

The reason comparing ourselves to others sabotages our happiness is simple: we immediately become ungrateful. Jealousy nixes gratitude. So how can you turn this kind of negative comparison around? For starters, you can stop looking for unfavorable comparisons. But it's often not enough to just stop doing that. We have to substitute our negative comparison with a positive one. In other words, we need to consider people who don't have it as well as we do. The instant you realize how blessed you are in comparison to some (whether it be with health, wealth, or family) is the instant your gratitude quotient increases and dissatisfaction dissipates. And if you want to multiply your positive emotion, reach out to those who are not doing as well as you are and you're sure to safeguard yourselves against negative comparisons.

> Everyone wants to live on top of the mountain, but all the happiness and growth occurs while you're climbing it.
>
> *Andy Rooney*

Oh, and one more thing. If you're sometimes guilty of the look-at-me impulse (on Facebook or otherwise), here's your litmus test: Would you still engage in this experience or buy what you're buying if you could tell no one about it?

Holding On to Pride

The *Wall Street Journal* ran a list of their best relationship columns from 2012, and the "Divorcé's Guide to Marriage" topped their list. It was based on a simple premise: if you want a great marriage, talk to a divorced person about what went wrong in their marriage. The article stated, "Research shows that most divorced people identify the same top regrets or behaviors they believe contributed to their marriage's demise and that they resolve to change next time. One researcher said, 'Divorced individuals who step back and say, 'This is what I've done wrong and this is what I will change,' have something powerful to teach others."

The number one lesson learned by divorced people? Forty-one percent said they would communicate differently. That is, they would learn to argue in a way that produces a solution, not just more anger and conflict. In short, they would let go of their pride and approach their partner with more humility as best they could.

The Bible makes it plain: "Pride leads to conflict."[6] A prideful spirit keeps couples from cooperating, flexing, respecting, compromising, and resolving. Instead it fuels defensiveness and discord. It stands in the way of saying "I'm sorry." Self-centered pride is sure to steal happiness from any marriage.

Research shows that when pride sets in, a partner will continue an argument 34 percent of the time even if he knows he's wrong—or can't remember what the fight was about. And a full 74 percent will fight on even if they feel "it's a losing battle."[7] Is it any wonder that pride is a saboteur of happiness?

> Plenty of people miss their share of happiness, not because they never found it, but because they didn't stop to enjoy it.
>
> *William Feather*

Pride has a way of secretly seeping into the crevices of our conversations even when we are consciously inclined to avoid it. That's what makes it so toxic and devious. "Through pride we are ever deceiving ourselves," said Carl Jung. "But deep down below the surface of the average conscience a still, small voice says to us, something is out of tune."

You know the feeling of being out of tune. We all do. It's born of the tension between being the kind of person we want to be and our fear of being snookered. We don't want to be prideful, but we also don't want to be duped. That's what causes pride to kick in. And that's when we realize, deep down, that we've taken the low road. And more often than not, this sinking feeling becomes too difficult to admit to ourselves, let alone our spouse, so we perpetuate our pride.

The antidote to unhealthy pride is, of course, humility. And the word from which we get *humility* literally means "from the earth." In other words, humility steps off its high horse to be common and lowly. Humility isn't for cowards. It's risky. Humility makes us vulnerable to being played or made to look the fool. But it also makes possible everything else we truly want to be. William Gurnall said, "Humility is the necessary veil to all other graces." Without humility, it's nearly impossible to engender kindness and warmth with our spouse. Without humility it's impossible to find happiness in marriage.

Obsessing Over the Past

Your present is inextricably linked to your past. If you are weighed down by regret, pain, and guilt over things that happened two decades ago or two hours ago, you will not be able to live fully in the present. As long as you're perpetually gazing over your shoulder, you will feel unfinished. You will feel distracted. You will feel less alive than you are. Your past will seep into your present and contaminate almost every one of your thoughts, feelings, and actions. And the attention you give to your past can't help but distract from your marriage.

This isn't our opinion. It's a fact. Unfinished business takes on a life of its own because the brain remembers incomplete tasks or failures longer than any success or completed activity. It's technically referred to as the *Zeigarnik effect*.[8] When a project or a thought is completed, the

> I am more and more convinced that our happiness depends more on how we meet the events in our lives, than on those events themselves.
>
> *Alexander Humboldt*

brain places it in a special memory. The brain no longer gives the project priority or active working status, and bits and pieces of the achieved situation begin to decay. But regrets have no closure. The brain continues to spin the memory, trying to come up with ways to fix the mess and move it from active to inactive status. But it can't—not without our deliberate help.

So if your pain or regrets from the past are sabotaging your happiness in the present, start by focusing on where it hurts. This includes getting over jealousy of your partner's past relationships, irritation at how your mother-in-law treats you, something from your own childhood that makes it hard for you to trust, a spat you had with your spouse six months ago.

Healing your hurts, particularly if they run deep, will likely bring closure to many parts of your past. Be aware, however, that healing your hurts is a process of self-exploration. It can be painful. Personal growth almost always is. It can also feel lonely. This is work you need to do on your own. Your spouse can be supportive but they can't do the work for you. But no matter how painful and lonely the process, it's worth the price.

Fixating on the Future

When we were both working on our doctorates, we had a little quote we framed and put on the wall where we did most of our studying. It said: "Some people spend their entire lives indefinitely preparing to live." This single sentence reminded us not to put life on hold while we were working so hard to earn our degrees. After all, it's tempting to say things like, "Once we graduate, we'll start to have fun" or "Once we get a house, we can really start living" or "Once we get that job, we can relax."

This mentality of putting life on hold is tempting for people who are goal oriented. And it's just as tempting for dreamers who think about their goals but never achieve them. In both cases their happiness waits for them in the future. Either way, this future-looking mind-set can impair happiness. So if you're too busy making plans for the future to live more fully in the present, take heed. Life is here and now—not there and then.

Maybe you've heard this little poem. It makes such a simple but profound point:

> Each morning he stacked up the letters he'd write
> Tomorrow.
> And think of the folks he would fill with delight
> Tomorrow.
> It was too bad, indeed, he was busy today,
> And hadn't a minute to stop on his way;
> More time he would have to give others he'd say
> Tomorrow.
> The greatest of workers this man would have been
> Tomorrow.
> The world would have known him, had he ever seen
> Tomorrow.
> But the fact is he died and he faded from view,
> And all that he left here when living was through
> Was a mountain of things he intended to do
> Tomorrow.[9]

Do you ever fear ending up like the man in the poem, who died while waiting for the future? Do you ever feel as if you're waiting for your life to begin? Don't spend your life preparing to live. Do your best to live in the present. Now is the time. Happiness need not be put on hold.

Giving In to the Silver Medal Syndrome

If you're a fan of the Olympic Games, you know that the athletes focus their entire lives on being the best they can be. Their discipline is legendary. They keep to a strict regimen of working out and practicing as if their life depended on it. They limit their diets to include the perfect blend of protein, fiber, complex carbohydrates, and nutrients. Why? To medal. Winning a medal is what it's all about. It drives every Olympian.

But not all medals are created equal. Researchers surveyed the happiness of the gold, silver, and bronze medal winners. The happiest? No surprise. Gold, of course. But the next result may surprise you. You may think the silver medalists were next on the happiness scale. They weren't. The bronze medalists were happier than the silver medalists.

The silver medalists think, *I came so close to winning gold.* The bronze medalists think, *I almost didn't get a medal—I'm grateful to be on the podium.* One reflects on what they have, the other reflects on what they don't have. The third-place athlete is happier than the second-place athlete. The bronze medalists even smile more than the silver winners on the podium at the medal ceremony.[10]

It's known as the *Silver Medal Syndrome*[11] and, sadly, we all sometimes suffer from it. It happens anytime we reflect on how something might have turned out better. We play the "if only" game: "If only we would have invested in that business." "If only we hadn't moved here." "If only you were more romantic." It's tempting to want more rather than be grateful for what we have. And whenever we focus on what we don't have rather than what we do, happiness wanes.

There you have it, five hazards that are worth watching as you do your best to make happy together: (1) unfavorable comparisons to others, (2) holding onto pride, (3) obsessing over the past, (4) fixating on the future, and (5) giving into the silver medal syndrome. Before we leave you in this chapter, however, we have one more suggestion.

> I must learn to be content with being happier than I deserve.
>
> *Jane Austen*

The Best Predictor of a Happy Marriage

Harvard psychology professor Daniel Gilbert, after reviewing a massive well-being index, stated "Americans are smiling less and worrying more . . . happiness is down and sadness is up . . . and depression is on the rise." Why? He summed it up in a single word: uncertainty. It's one of the great hazards to happiness. When people don't know what's going to happen it's tough to be content. Whether it's uncertainty about employment, the economy, international conflict, or social and political issues, uncertainty breeds dissatisfaction.

A couple of studies underscore the point, according to Professor Gilbert. In a Dutch experiment, some subjects were told they would be intensely shocked twenty times at regular intervals. The researchers told a second group they would receive three strong shocks and seventeen mild ones, but they wouldn't know when the intense shocks would come. The results? Subjects in the second group sweated more and experienced faster heart rates. Uncertainty caused their discomfort; they didn't know when the shocks would come next.

Another study showed that colostomy patients who knew that their colostomies would be permanent were happier six months after their procedures than those who were told there might be a chance of reversing their colostomies. Once again, uncertainty caused the unhappiness.

Daniel Gilbert summarized, "An uncertain future leaves us stranded in an unhappy present with nothing to do but wait."[12] The anxiety of waiting on an undefined future can't help but hinder happiness—especially in marriage. That's why the most important thing any couple can do to ensure happiness together is to build a rock-solid relationship. When you have a love you can count on—an enduring love—it soothes the anxiety of all other uncertainties.

Chances are you've read 1 Corinthians 13 numerous times. It's quoted at countless weddings. In fact, it's the most quoted passage of Scripture around the world. The Love Chapter, as it is known, reveals the ideal love everyone yearns for. But something about these words, the way they are written, tells us they are meant to be not only admired but also lived. These words are a means to a more excellent way of living.

> The activity of happiness must occupy an entire lifetime; for one swallow does not a summer make.
>
> *Aristotle*

While the passage draws a profile of ideal love, it is too plainly spoken to be a mere mystical flight of fancy. Paul, the writer of these words, was surely inspired as he penned them. Love is patient. Love is kind. It is not jealous, does not get angry quickly. These are qualities ordinary people can cultivate to build extraordinary relationships.

And when any Bible translator nears the close of Paul's love poem he must feel the gravity of the final quality: love endures. Note that love doesn't simply survive, as noble as that may sometimes be. Paul has more in mind than hanging on. Enduring is not a passive act. It calls for courage to conquer whatever may keep us from moving forward. It calls for strength. The word *endurance*, in fact, is Irish in origin and literally means "oak wood"—one of the strongest and most enduring of timbers.

Here's how J. B. Phillips translated it: "Love knows no limit to its endurance, no end to its trust, no fading of its hope; it can outlast anything. It is, in fact, the one thing that still stands when all else has fallen."

> A happy marriage is the union of two good forgivers.
> *Ruth Bell Graham*

It's fitting that Paul's list of love's qualities concludes with perseverance. For it is only after we have worked to cultivate patience, kindness, hope, and all the rest that we truly recognize the wisdom found in love's power to endure.

Ask any couple who has been happily married for fifty years if their love life was a cakewalk. You'll be hard pressed to find one who says so. Sure, many seasoned couples focus their memories on the positive side, but every lifelong couple who can look back over the decades together has endured tough times. You can be sure of that. They are happy not because of their circumstances but in spite of them. And you can be sure of one other thing: they persevered, not because of legal or social constraints, but because love endures to the last.

And that—that certainty of love—makes all the difference in finding happiness together.

For Reflection

1. Do you ever feel that you may be missing out on the joy of happiness because you're so focused on pursuing it? If so, when and in what ways?

2. Of the five potential hazards of happiness covered in this chapter, which one is most likely to trip you up? How? Why?

3. Do you agree that a rock-solid marriage, a love that endures, a relationship you can count on goes a long way in soothing the anxiety that comes from so many of life's uncertainties? What's a personal example you can think of?

10 Your Three-Week Happiness Plan

> Action may not always bring happiness, but there is no happiness without action.
>
> *William James*

ABOUT THREE BLOCKS FROM our home in downtown Seattle is the flagship store for Recreational Equipment, Inc., commonly known as REI. It has a three-story climbing rock just inside its front doors where customers stand in line to try out their climbing equipment. The structure has captivated our two boys since they were toddlers. And, no, neither of their parents has ever considered climbing it.

But not long ago the two of us happened to meet Jim Whittaker, a former CEO of REI and the first American to summit Mount Everest. We were invited to a talk he was giving about his historic climb, recounting the day he reached the summit and planted a US flag at the top of the world's highest mountain. And if there was one single message we came away with from his remarks it was this:

scaling Mount Everest takes a massive amount of preparation. It takes a well-formed plan.

To begin with you need gear. Like no fewer than three separate pairs of boots: double plastic climbing boots, fully insulated over-boots, and light hiking boots. Plus socks. Wool socks, pile socks, synthetic socks. And that's just for starters. There are climbing harnesses, trekking poles, ice axes, and on and on. There is the issue of food and water. Weather predictions need to be studied. And we haven't even gotten to all of the physical preparation your body needs before you set foot on the mountain.

> Happiness is a choice that requires effort at times.
>
> *Aeschylus*

You get the point. A major adventure like climbing Everest requires a plan. Thankfully, achieving a higher level of happiness in your marriage will not require buying any gear. It won't demand physical training or a strict diet. So relax. The plan we want to help you develop in this chapter is painless. That's not to say it won't take work on your part, but it's doable.

You will come away from this chapter with a personalized and concrete plan for infusing your marriage with deeper joy and more happiness. So unhook your carabiners and put your feet up. This is going to be easier than you think.

Your Happiness Pie: A Quick Reminder

As you recall from early on in this book, 50 percent of our happiness is determined by our biological set point and 10 percent by our circumstances. It's the 40 percent of the happiness pie that is completely under our control.[1] It's determined by our choices and has nothing to do with our genetic makeup or our circumstances. Happy people and happy couples are literally making happy by deciding to. They are being intentional. They are making smart choices that boost their well-being together. And that's exactly what your three-week happiness plan is going to help you do.

As we promised from the start, your happiness plan won't cost more money. And it won't consume inordinate amounts of time. The plan is incredibly doable and it is guaranteed to help you live at a level of happiness that surpasses your natural set point.

Does the Plan Really Work?

You might be wondering how we know that a plan like this can actually work. Well, training your brain to be more upbeat and your relationship to be more positive is not so different from training your muscles at the gym. Recent research on neuroplasticity—the ability of the brain to change even in adulthood—reveals that as you develop new habits you rewire your brain.[2] So if you're wondering whether a simple happiness plan can actually work, the answer is yes.

Consider a happiness plan that distinguished Harvard professor Shawn Achor gave to a group of tax managers in New York to see if it could help them be happier during their busy tax season—a time of year when they are least happy.[3] He simply had them choose to do one of five activities that correlate with positive change every day for three weeks.

Several days after the training concluded, he evaluated both the participants and a control group

> Rules for Happiness: something to do, someone to love, something to hope for.
>
> *Immanuel Kant*

to determine their general sense of well-being. On every metric, the experimental group's scores were significantly higher than the control group's. When he tested both groups again, four months later, the experimental group still showed significantly higher scores in life satisfaction. In fact, participants' mean score on the life satisfaction scale—a metric widely accepted to be one of the greatest predictors of productivity and happiness at work—moved from 22.96 on a 35-point scale before the training to 27.23 four months later, a significant increase.

Just one quick exercise a day kept these tax managers happier for months after the training program had ended. Happiness had become habitual.

The same will be true for the two of you as you put into motion a plan that requires just one action each day for twenty-one days.

Get the Most from Your Happiness Plan

We've got a terrific tool for helping you put your happiness plan into action—it's far more robust than what we can do in a book. It includes:

- video messages from us to you
- daily inspirational quotes
- a cheat sheet of reminders to help you succeed
- a printable booklet you can customize for your plan

You'll find it all at www.MakingHappyBook.com

Your Twenty-One-Day Happiness Plan

The following gives you an overview of the plan that you'll find in a more robust and user-friendly format on our Web site. But just in case you don't have an online connection, we wanted to provide this for you here. In fact, you may want to peruse the whole plan before you jump into the first day. But once you're ready, we suggest going full force. Don't treat this like a shopping list. The value comes in stretching beyond your comfort level in various places. That means doing some things that you might not immediately lean into. So when you're ready, make the commitment—to yourself, to each other, and to the three-week plan.

DAY 1: START A GRATITUDE JOURNAL

Feel free to do this on your own, but we suggest doing this together. Use a little notebook that you can trade back and forth. One of you writes three things he or she is grateful for today. They can be anything, but we suggest that one of the three be related to something specific in your relationship or about your spouse. Once the first partner has noted three things he or she is grateful for the notebook can be left for the other partner to do the same. You'll be using this again in your three-week plan, but that's it for now.

See chapter 3 for a refresher.

DAY 2: HAVE A DREAM TALK

Set aside at least twenty minutes at some point today to talk about your future together. Ideally you'll do this without distraction (turn off phones if you can). Imagine yourself years down the road in as much detail as possible. Consider different time increments. For example, where do you see yourselves and your relationship in one year, five years, ten, and so on. What goals will you have accomplished? What worries will be squelched? What mental images can you both conjure that represent something energizing about your future together? Beware: dream talks typically start off slow and gain momentum as you go. Also, look ahead to Day 5 and start making plans for it today.

See chapter 5 for a refresher.

DAY 3: JOIN YOUR SPIRITS WITH A MEANINGFUL MEDITATION

Begin or end your day with a devotion reading or a meditation that you can share. There are countless places to find something like this to read together. If you'd like, you can use our free online weekly devotional, *Couple to Couple,* by going to www.lesandleslie.com/devotions. It will take you less than ten minutes to read a little meditation together and discuss it. Be sure to focus on being fully present for this brief experience. If you're just doing it to "check it off your list," you're wasting your time. Put your heart into it and you'll soon see why this can be so valuable to your relationship.

See chapter 7 for a refresher.

DAY 4: MAKE A LIST OF
FIFTY KIND ACTS YOU CAN SHARE TOGETHER

Later on in your three-week happiness plan you'll be doing some kind acts you can share together. But today we're simply asking you to formulate your list of possibilities. Believe us, this will be a bit of a challenge at first. Why? Because we want you to list fifty specific actions you can do together that demonstrate a new and special act of kindness beyond your relationship. We say "new and special" because you're already doing acts of kindness even if you're not thinking much about it. This list is dedicated to new actions—big and small.

See chapter 8 for a refresher.

DAY 5: DO AN UNEXPECTED DATE

Do you recall reading about the power of doing something novel on a date together and how it can revive passion and connection in your relationship? Well, tonight's the night. We gave you a warning a few days ago, so hopefully you have something in store for this evening that you've never done before. Whether it's driving go-carts or picking cherries or taking a cooking class together, the point is to make your shared experience novel. That's the key. A dinner and a movie won't cut it for this date.

By the way, you'll be doing one more of these before your three-week plan is done so you may want to each take one of the date nights and surprise your partner with what you're doing. Either way, have fun!

See chapter 4 for a refresher.

DAY 6: DO SHARED SERVICE IN SECRET

Okay. The day before yesterday you made a long list of things you could do together to show kindness to others. Review that list today and select one item from the list that the two of you can do to help someone else—and do it today in secret. That is, don't tell anyone else you're doing it or that you've done it. If possible, do your kindness without the recipient even knowing it was from you. The goal is to make this act of kindness something that only the two of you know about. So get sneaky with your service.

See chapter 8 for a refresher.

DAY 7: EXCHANGE YOUR GRATITUDE JOURNAL

Seven days ago you each noted three specific things you were grateful for. It's time to do this again. But this time be sure to make at least one note of another person or couple who has inspired you or helped you in your own marriage. It could be a family member, a minister, a friend, or even a counselor. You can each do this on your own if you like and then share and discuss what you wrote later in the day.

See chapter 3 for a refresher.

DAY 8: BUILD A BUCKET LIST

Today you're going to brainstorm together about all of the things you'd like to achieve, accomplish, or experience on this planet. Whether it's a place you'd like to visit, an activity you'd like to do, or even a person you'd like to meet, put it on your list. This is your chance to focus on the frivolous, for the most part. Your bucket list doesn't need to be deep or meaningful. But make it long and discard any ideas if they sound good to only one you. This will be a list that creates some of your most memorable experiences. Don't try to impress anyone. Make the list for yourselves. After you build your list, keep it in a place where you can both refer to it.

Also, you may want to look ahead to tomorrow's action and begin thinking about it today—just in case you need to do any advanced planning.

See chapter 5 for a refresher.

DAY 9: START A DREAM BOARD

A few days ago you had a dream talk. And more recently you made a bucket list. Today you're going to revisit both of them and make them more tangible by creating a dream board. This may sound gimmicky, but hear us out. Research shows that if you have a place to view visible reminders of your goals and dreams, you are far more likely to realize them. So make a dream board together. You can make it electronically (with an app) or go old school. Either way, you simply collect images and pictures that remind you of your dream. Search for photos online. Cut images out of old magazines. Wherever you get your pictures, do it together today and talk about the images as you're creating your display. Place the board where you can both revisit it from time to time and continue to add to it. Today is just the start, so don't feel that it's a one-day definitive project.

See chapter 5 for a refresher.

DAY 10: PLAN A GRATITUDE VISIT

Are you ready for this one? It's perhaps the most challenging of actions on your three-week plan—but probably the most rewarding. Five days from now we're going to ask you to visit another person or couple who has been particularly meaningful to both of you and has helped you. In preparation for this meeting, we want you to begin today by writing a one-page testimonial expressing what that person or couple has done for you and how grateful you are for the good they brought into your lives. Take your time to craft an especially heartfelt letter.

We want you to also arrange an in-person meeting with the individual or couple if at all possible (it's far more significant than doing it by e-mail or phone) in five days' time (see Day 15). So you'll want to arrange your schedules accordingly for that. Don't tell them what the meeting is for. Just tell them you'd like an hour of their time and you'll explain when you arrive.

See chapter 3 for a refresher.

DAY 11: CONCENTRATE YOUR KINDNESS TO OTHERS TOGETHER

You may recall that research reveals when you focus several acts of kindness together within a single day you are bound to get a significant emotional uplift. So here's your assignment today: each of you will make your own individual lists of five things you will do today to add value to others or simply perform acts of kindness. They may not be major actions but they will be new. If you normally hold the door open for strangers at the grocery, don't put that on your list. These will be new acts of kindness for you. Some may be for friends or colleagues. Some may be for complete strangers. The key is for each of you to do all five acts of kindness today (on your own) and then share your experiences together this evening.

See chapter 8 for a refresher.

DAY 12: DO AN UNEXPECTED DATE

Okay. It's time for another innovative date night. If one of you was in charge of the last one a week ago, the other partner is in charge of this one. Just as before, the key is novelty—doing something the two of you haven't done before or at least haven't done in an awfully long time. So get crazy and have a blast. Oh, and look ahead to tomorrow's assignment. You may want to do some advance planning or at the very least some anticipating.

See chapter 4 for a refresher.

DAY 13: CREATE SOME HOT MONOGAMY

Tonight you're scheduling a romantic and passionate encounter in your bedroom—or maybe somewhere else if that's what you're into. We want you to look forward to this all day long. You may want to provide each other with a sexy little gift or perhaps a nice candle to set the mood. And speaking of mood, don't forget some music. The point is to make tonight's lovemaking more than just routine. It's going to be special. That means you need to romanticize each other all day long.

By the way, if scheduling this sort of thing seems to take the romance out of it for you, then you probably haven't been married too long. Any seasoned couple knows how special and exciting a scheduled night of hot monogamy can be.

See chapter 4 for a refresher.

DAY 14: EXCHANGE YOUR GRATITUDE JOURNAL

It's time once again for each of you to note three things you are grateful for today. It's been a week since you did this. So this time we want you to make all three of your expressions of gratitude in your journal specifically about your partner. Be as detailed as possible. And of course, when you're ready, let your partner read what you have written.

See chapter 3 for a refresher.

DAY 15: COMPLETE YOUR GRATITUDE VISIT

Okay. You knew this day was coming and here you are. You're both going to visit the person or couple you wrote the letter to on Day 10. You've already arranged to meet them today. So here's the deal: when you arrive, explain why you are both there and that you've written a letter you want to read to them. Read your testimonial of gratitude aloud to them. Read slowly, with expression, and with eye contact, allowing the other person to react unhurriedly. You may want to each read different portions of your letter aloud to them. That's up to you. Focus on being fully present. Don't be embarrassed. They will be so honored by your action. And you will feel so great to express such heartfelt gratitude to someone who has added value to your marriage. Of course you'll want to leave the letter with them, so be sure to keep a copy for yourselves.

See chapter 3 for a refresher.

DAY 16: REVISIT YOUR DREAM TALK AND DREAM BOARD

Seven days ago you made a dream board together. Take just a few moments at some point today to look at it again together and identify which picture is most exciting to you. Explain why. Which item do you both think is the one you are most likely to achieve the soonest? What can you do today that will bring you a step closer to realizing it? The point in revisiting your dreams is to instill the habit of talking about them frequently. That keeps hope alive. And hope is essential for making your dreams a reality.

See chapter 5 for a refresher.

DAY 17: SELECT A SONG FOR YOUR PARTNER

Today we want each of you to play a song for each other. Don't worry, you don't have to be musical for this (but if you are you can certainly sing to your partner). Think of it as being like one of the old dedications you've heard on the radio. But in this case it's much more personal and intimate. In this case you're going to play the song for your partner (from your playlist), but before you do, explain why you selected this particular song for them on this particular day. You may even ask them to hold your hand while it plays. You don't need to play the songs back to back. You can choose to play your song for your partner whenever you think the time is right today. You might play your song for your partner in the morning. Your partner might play his or her song for you in the evening. You get the idea.

See chapter 6 for a refresher.

DAY 18: INITIATE A MENTORING RELATIONSHIP

One of the most significant ways to add value to others as a couple is by mentoring a less experienced couple. That is, coming alongside them and allowing them to learn from your successes as well as your challenges. Have you ever considered doing this for another couple? You might think it sounds a bit presumptuous, but more than likely there are couples within your sphere of influence that would love to have you invest in them. It doesn't need to take much of your time and it can even be short term. Marriage mentoring has proven to be such an effective happiness boost to couples that we want you to give it serious consideration today. You can learn more by going to MarriageMentoring.com. Watch the two-minute video that casts a vision for this effort and discuss.

See chapter 8 for a refresher.

DAY 19: DO AN UNEXPECTED DATE

Here we are at your third date night in this three-week happiness plan. You know the drill by now. Keep it innovative. If you're already running out of ideas, consult your friends. Search the Web. Look for discounts and coupons. After experiencing two unexpected and innovative dates already, we know you see the value in keeping it fresh. So tonight we want to let you off the hook if need be. If you'd get just as much fun and enjoyment out of a more routine date tonight, go for it. There's nothing wrong with dinner and a movie. And a date night is always a good thing. But if you've got the energy, we still urge you to keep it fresh.

See chapter 4 for a refresher.

DAY 20: HELP A NEEDY CHILD

Few things will give your relationship more of a boost than reaching out to a child who can benefit from your help. This might be a child at a local shelter whom you've never met or a child you know from church or somewhere else. But today we want to you help a needy child. If you're having a tough time identifying a child in need, call a local shelter or church outreach. They'll surely know how to guide you. And you may even want to consider sponsoring a needy child in another country through a relief organization like World Vision. They make it easy and meaningful. And as the advertisements say, it truly is less than the price of a cup of coffee a day to change a child's life forever. Regardless of what you do, dedicate this day to improving the life of a child together.

See chapter 8 for a refresher.

DAY 21: PRAY IT FORWARD

On this final day of your three-week happiness plan, we suggest that you simply pray a prayer of thanksgiving together. Whether you pray aloud together, write your prayers down, or simply pray silently together, give thanks to God. Before you do this, however, we also recommend that you recount your past twenty days and discuss your highlights. How would you assess the happiness you made together? Can you see a notable increase in well-being and joy together? What stands out for you? What would you like to keep doing together and how can you make it a routine? After giving a few minutes to your discussion, simply pray a prayer of thanksgiving and ask God to direct your next steps as you move forward.

See chapter 7 for a refresher.

For Reflection

1. As you review the list of Happiness Boosters from Part Two of the book (count your blessings, try new things, dream a dream, celebrate each other, attune your spirits, and add value to others), which one of them seems most challenging for you and why?

2. As you consider starting your three-week happiness plan, what is likely to keep you from following through with it? What can you do at this point to keep that from hindering you?

3. What was the most surprising or helpful piece of information you discovered while reading this book and why?

Happily Ever After?

It is only possible to live happily ever after on a day to day basis.

Margaret Bonnano

WE WERE STANDING IN a medieval courtyard in Lucerne, Switzerland. Six-story buildings from the 1500s surrounded us, including the old city hall clock tower. We were taking photos like most tourists and looking for a place to have lunch. "Look at this old apothecary shop," Les said. He was pointing to a building sandwiched in between other structures that might have been no more than twenty feet wide. The first two floors of the building's façade were stone and featured two arched windows on the main floor, along with a door. The upper portion of the façade displayed a weathered but meticulous painting of a tree and the crests of its former inhabitants.

Jutting just a bit out of the second floor was a tiny bay window with a Latin inscription painted above it: *amor medicabilis nvllis herbis.* We had our photo snapped in front of it and headed off to lunch.

Back home in Seattle, as we reviewed our photos, we became curious about the Latin phrase on this ancient pharmacy and had it translated. It's meaning? "No medicine can cure love."

Think of that. Even back in the 1500s they knew that love was a sickness. It's true. Love, that one one-syllable word as heavy as a heartbeat, spins our head. We become irrational. We become "sick with love." Or as Shakespeare put it, "Love is merely a madness." But maybe that's not all bad, at least at the beginning. According to a study published recently in the journal *Psychological Science*, the happiest newlyweds are the ones that are the most, well, delusional.

> There is only one happiness in life, to love and be loved.
>
> *George Sands*

The study followed 222 newlywed couples for three years. The respondents were asked to rate their marriage, as well as themselves and their partners in various areas including intelligence, creativity, and athletic skills. Researchers compared the self-ratings of each participant with the spouse's ratings and found that those who had an inflated view of their partners also rated their marriages as happier. In fact, those who had an abnormally high level of rose-colored-glasses mentality about each other were the only pairs who didn't show a decline in their level of marriage happiness. "People who were the most idealistic about their partner in the beginning showed no decline at all in satisfaction over the first three years of marriage," said study lead author Sandra Murray, psychology professor at the State University of New York.[1]

But here's the rub: most of us don't wear rose-colored glasses for long in our marriage. We come to realize that our partner is less than ideal. They don't always make us happy.

So hear this: we will never be happy or fulfilled until we stop measuring our real-life relationship against the dream of whatever we imagined would make us happy. It's what Daniel Levinson called the "tyranny of the dream."[2] The seeds of this dream were planted before we even met our partner. We nurtured it through our own imaginings. And the dream was to marry someone truly special and live happily ever after.

But inevitably, of course, our rose-colored glasses come off because we're *not* delusional. Marriage isn't what we imagined or dreamed. Our fairytale relationship on occasion may even feel more like a nightmare.

If only our partner would think, feel, and do better, we say to ourselves, *we might have a chance at true happiness*. But, as Anias Nin reminds us, "We've been poisoned by fairytales." They don't come true. The dream can never make us happy. Because the early onset of delusional love doesn't last. We eventually sober up from love's elixir. It may take three years. It may take more. But our dream of idealized love doesn't last. And if we keep measuring reality against it, we will be forever unhappy.

Our delusional dream is a shallow and selfish hope anyway. As we said at the outset, marriage is not designed to make you happy—you are designed to make your marriage happy. Our greatest hope for happiness is far deeper than a

> It is only possible to live happily ever after on a daily basis.
>
> *Margaret Bonanno*

self-absorbed dream. Our greatest hope for happiness is found in meaning that transcends pleasure. And we find this kind of meaning in marriage when we love without self-interest and sometimes sacrificially. This is the secret of living happily ever after.

Acknowledgments

Byron Williamson, President and Publisher of Worthy, is a delight to work with. So is Jeana Ledbetter, our editorial expert. Leslie Peterson and Kyle Olund polished every sentence. We are grateful to our entire the sales, marketing and publicity team: Dennis Disney, Morgan Canclini, Alyson White, Betty Woodmancy, Sherrie Slopianka, and Troy Johnson. We appreciate the expertise of Eddie Thornhill and Kelli Douglas in production, who helped get this book in print. And thanks also to those at Worthy who work so hard behind the scenes, David Howell, Susan Thomas, and Margaret Brock. We could not be more grateful to the entire Worthy family for allowing us to publish with them.

As always, we owe a huge debt to Sealy Yates. We couldn't ask for a better agent or friend. Mandi Moragne, our Director of Awesome Customer Experiences, cares about the people we serve every bit as much as we do. Janice Lundquist has managed our life on the road (and more) in a way that two travelers have no right to expect or ask. Kevin Small, the chair of our nonprofit, is incredibly helpful at every turn. And Ryan Farmer, along with his wife, Kendra, are unimaginable gifts to our efforts. Ryan helps us uphold a standard of excellence without ever flinching and adds value to everything he touches. We could not be more grateful to him and our entire team who have worked so hard on our behalf. We owe you a million thanks.

About the Authors

Drs. Les and Leslie Parrott are #1 *New York Times* best-selling authors and the founders of the Center for Relationship Development at Seattle Pacific University (SPU). Les is a psychologist and Leslie is a marriage and family therapist at SPU. The Parrotts are authors of *The Good Fight, Crazy Good Sex, L.O.V.E. Your Time-Starved Marriage, Love Talk,* and the Gold Medallion Award-winning *Saving Your Marriage Before It Starts.* The Parrotts have been featured on *Oprah, CBS This Morning,* CNN, and *The View,* and in *USA Today* and the *New York Times.* They are also frequent guest speakers and have written for a variety of magazines. The Parrotts' Web site, **LesandLeslie.com**, features more than one thousand free video-on-demand pieces answering relationship questions. Les and Leslie live in Seattle, Washington, with their two sons.

Notes

INTRODUCTION:
HOOKED ON A FEELING

1. R. E. Lucas, "Adaptation and the Set-Point Model of Subjective Well-being: Does Happiness Change after Major Life Events?" *Current Directions in Psychological Science* 16, no. 2 (2007): 75–80.

2. In recent years, our happiness levels in general have not risen. They've even decreased from previous generations. In spite of an increased standard of living, more entertainment options than ever, and countless conveniences that were unimaginable just a few years ago, we are experiencing what researchers call "static happiness." [Kessler, R. C., McGonagle, K. A. Zhao, S., Nelson, C. B., Hughes, M., Eshlman, S., Wittchen, H. U., and Kendler, K. S. (1994). Lifetime and 12-month prevalence rates of DSM-III-R psychiatric disorders in the United States: Results from the National Comorbidity Survey. Archives of General Psychiatry, 51: 8–19.] In the 1940s, when people were asked, "How happy are you?" the average score was 7.7 out of 10. Most recently, the average score was 7.2 out of 10. [Holly J. Morris, "Happiness Explained," U.S. News & World Report (9-03-01), pp. 46-54] The Gallup Well-Being Index shows that Americans are "smiling less and worrying more" than in previous years. [Gilbert, Daniel, "What You Don't Know Makes You Nervous," The New York Times (May 21, 2009).] Sadness and depression are on the rise. In part, this is the kind of information that led us to write this book.

CHAPTER 1:

LET THE HAPPINESS BEGIN

1. Matt Mabe, "They Teach Happiness at Harvard," *Bloomberg Businessweek*, August 20, 2008, http://www.businessweek.com/stories/2008-08-20/they-teach-happiness-at-harvardbusinessweek-business-news-stock-market-and-financial-advice.

2. Martin Seligman, quoted in Rob Hirtz, "Martin Seligman's Journey from Learned Helplessness to Learned Happiness," *The Pennsylvania Gazette*, (January-February 1998), http://www.upenn.edu/gazette/0199/hirtz.html.

3. Seligman defines positive psychology as "the scientific study of positive human functioning and flourishing on multiple levels that include the biological, personal, relational, institutional, cultural, and global dimensions of life. Martin E. P. Seligman and Mihaly Csikszentmihalyi "Positive Psychology: An Introduction," *American Psychologist* 55, no. 1 (2000): 5–14.

4. Corey L. M. Keyes and Shane Lopez, "Toward a Science of Mental Health: Positive Directions in Diagnosis and Interventions," (2002), quoted in C. R. Snyder and Shane J. Lopez , eds., *Handbook of Positive Psychology* (New York: Oxford University Press, 2011), 45–59.

5. William C. Compton and Edward Hoffman. *Positive Psychology: The Science of Happiness and Flourishing,* 2nd ed. (Belmont, CA: Wadsworth Cengage Learning, 2013).

6. Richard J. Davidson and Sharon Begley, *The Emotional Life of Your Brain: How Its Unique Patterns Affect the Way You Think, Feel, and Live—and How You Can Change Them* (New York: Hudson Street Press, 2012).

7. Jonathan Haidt and Jesse Graham, "When Morality Opposes Justice: Conservatives Have Moral Intuitions That Liberals May Not Recognize," *Social Justice Research* 20, no. 1 (2007): 98–116.

8. Paul J. Zak, Angela A. Stanton, and Sheila Ahmadi, "Oxytocin Increases Generosity in Humans," (2007), PLoS ONE 2(11): e1128. doi:10.1371/journal.pone.0001128. Jorge A. Barraza and Paul J. Zak, "Empathy toward Strangers Triggers Oxytocin Release and Subsequent Generosity," *Annals of the New York Academy of Sciences* 1167 (June 2009): 182–89.

9. Andrew J. Tomarken et al., "Individual Differences in Anterior Brain Asymmetry and Fundamental Dimensions of Emotion," *Journal of Personality and Social Psychology* 62, no. 4 (1992): 676–87. H. L. Urry et al., "Making a Life Worth Living: Neural Correlates of Well-being," *Psychological Science* 15, no. 6

(2004): 367–72. See also J. van Honk, and J. L. G. Schutter, "From Affective Valence to Motivational Direction: The Frontal Asymmetry of Emotion Revised," *Psychological Science* 17, no. 11 (2006): 963–65.

10. "The History of Happiness" by Peter N. Stearns; *Harvard Business Review*, January-February 2012.

11. Quote attributed to Catherine Marshall (1914–1983). Augustine wrote a whole book, *The Happy Life*, about human happiness. The ultimate goal of all human endeavor, he said, lies in happiness. Man can received happiness but not by satisfaction of goods of this world. Lasting happiness is possible only by living in God. God is the greatest happiness that a man can achieve, *"for God has created us to him and our heart is restless until it rests in God."*

12. John 15:11 msg.

CHAPTER 2:
DO YOU KNOW YOUR HAPPY FACTOR?

1. Philip Brickman, Dan Coates, Ronnie Janoff-Bulman, "Lottery Winners and Accident Victims: Is Happiness Relative?" *Journal of Personality and Social Psychology* 36, no. 8 (1978), http://education.ucsb.edu/janeconoley/ed197/documents/brickman_lotterywinnersandaccidentvictims.pdf.

2. Christian Seidl, Eva Camacho Cuena, Andrea Morone, "Income Distributions versus Lotteries Happiness, Response-Mode Effects, and Preference," Christian-Albrechts-University of Kiel, Department of Economics, no. 2003, 01, http://ideas.repec.org/p/zbw/cauewp/783.html.

3. Ed Diener, Jeff Horwitz, and Robert A. Emmons, "Happiness of the Very Wealthy." *Social Indicators Research* 16 (1985): 263–74.

4. Daniel Kahneman and Angus Deaton, "High Income Improves Evaluation of Life but Not Emotional Well-being." Proceedings of the National Academy of Sciences of the United States of America, 38-16489-16493 (2010).

5. Timothy D. Wilson and Daniel T. Gilbert, "Affective Forecasting: Knowing What to Want." *Current Directions in Psychological Science* 14, no. 3 (June 2005): 131–34. Daniel Gilbert. *Stumbling on Happiness.* (New York: Knopf, 2006).

6. Sonja Lyubomirsky, David Schkade, and Kennon M. Sheldon, "Pursuing Happiness: The Architecture of Sustainable Change," *Review of General Psychology* 9, no. 2 (2005): 111–31.

7. Quoted in Michael Mendelsohn, "Positive Psychology: The Science of Happiness," ABC News, January 11, 2008, http://abcnews.go.com/Health/story?id=4115033&page=1#.UWPfor8TH8.

8. Research suggests that a few events, chief among them being the unexpected death of a child and repeated bouts of unemployment seem to reduce our ability to be happy permanently. See Bruce Headey, "The Set Point Theory of Wellbeing Has Serious Flaws: On the Eve of a Scientific Revolution?" *Social Indicators Research* 97, no. 1 (2010): 7–21.

9. Sonja Lyubomirsky, *The How of Happiness: A Scientific Approach to Getting the Life You Want*. (New York: Penguin Press, 2008).

10. Marina Krakovsky, "The Science of Lasting Happiness," *Scientific American* (April 2007), http://www.scientificamerican.com/article.cfm?id=the-science-of-lasting-happiness.

11. Martin E. P. Seligman, *Authentic Happiness: Using the New Positive Psychology to Realize Your Potential for Lasting Fulfillment* (New York: Free Press, 2002).

12. "Short Takes: Gauging the impact of *Purpose Driven Life*, 10 years on," CNN Belief Blog (November 29, 2012), http://religion.blogs.cnn.com/2012/11/29/short-takes-gauging-the-impact-of-purpose-driven-life-10-years-on/.

13. "I have come that they may have life, and have it to the full." (John 10:10 NIV)

14. The Map of Happiness: World, http://www.mapofhappiness.com/world/.

15. Dan Buettner, *Thrive: Finding Happiness the Blue Zones Way* (New York: National Geographic Publishing, 2010).

16. Gallup Healthways (copyright, 2008), 2012 Gallup-Healthways Wellbeing Index, http://www.well-beingindex.com.

17. Ed Diener et al., "The Satisfaction with Life Scale, *Journal of Personality Assessment* 49 (January 10, 1985), http://ssrn.com/abstract=2199190.

18. "Is Happiness Contagious?" American Association for the Advancement of Science, (December 5, 2008), http://news.sciencemag.org/sciencenow/2008/12/05-01.html.

CHAPTER 3:
COUNT YOUR BLESSINGS

1. Adapted from YouTube.com, Louis CK, "Everything's Amazing and Nobody's Happy," February 2009.

2. Martin Greenberg, "A Theory of Indebtedness," in *Social Exchange: Advances in Theory and Research*, ed. Kenneth Gergen, Martin Greenberg and Richard Wills (New York: Plenum, 1980).

3. Robert A. Emmons and Teresa T. Kneezel, "Giving Gratitude: Spiritual and Religious Correlates of Gratitude" *Journal of Psychology and Christianity* 24 no.2 (2005): 140–48.

4. Michael McCullough, Robert Emmons, and Jo-Ann Tsang, "The Grateful Disposition: A Conceptual and Empirical Topography," *Journal of Personality and Social Psychology* 82, no. 1 (2002): 112–27.

5. Melinda Beck, "Thank You. No, Thank You," *Wall Street Journal*, November 23, 2010.

6. Amie M. Gordon, "Giving the Gift of Gratitude," *Psychology Today*, December 24, 2012, http://www.psychologytoday.com/blog/between-you-and-me/201212/giving-the-gift-gratitude.

7. Robert A. Emmons and Michael E. McCullough, "Counting Blessings Versus Burdens: Experimental Studies of Gratitude and Subjective Well-being in Daily Life," *Journal of Personality and Social Psychology* 84, no. 2 (2003): 377–89. See also Robert Emmons, *Thanks: How the New Science of Gratitude Can Make you Happier* (New York: Houghton Mifflin, 2009).

8. George Lewis, "Are Ya Kidding Me? No Complaints for 21 Days," *Today*, NBC.com, http://www.today.com/id/17362505/ns/today/t/are-ya-kidding-me-no-complaints-days/#.UY6q2pUTH8s.

9. Kennon M. Sheldon and Sonja Lyubomirsky, "How to Increase and Sustain Positive Emotion: The Effects of Expressing Gratitude and Visualizing Best Possible Selves," *The Journal of Positive Psychology* 1, no. 2 (2006): 73–82.

10. Michael E. McCullough, Jo-Ann Tsang, and Robert A. Emmons, "Gratitude in Intermediate Affective Terrain: Links of Grateful Moods with Individual Differences and Daily Emotional Experience," *Journal of Personality and Social Psychology* 86, no. 2 (2004): 295–309.

11. Martin E. P. Seligman et al., "Positive Psychology Progress: Empirical Validation of Interventions," *American Psychologist* 60, no. 5 (2005): 410–21.

12. Stephen King, *Lisey's Story* (New York: Scribner, 2006), 20–21.

CHAPTER 4:

TRY NEW THINGS

1. Daniel Kahneman et al., "A Survey Method for Characterizing Daily Life Experience: The Day Reconstruction Method," *Science* 306 (December 2004): 1776–80.

2. W. Richard Walker et al., "Why People Rehearse Their Memories: Frequency of Use and Relations to the Intensity of Emotions Associated with Autobiographical Memories," *Memory* 17, no. 7 (2009): 760–73.

3. W. Richard Walker, Rodney J. Vogl, and Hailee E. Brown, "The Role of Spreading Activation in the Retrieval of Autobiographical Memories," *International Journal of Humanities and Social Science* 1, no. 8 (2011): 54–63.

4. Bianca P. Acevedo et al., "Neural Correlates of Long-term Intense Romantic Love," *Social Cognitive and Affective Neuroscience* 7, no. 2 (2012): 145–59.

5. Arthur Aron et al., "Couples Shared Participation in Novel and Arousing Activities and Experienced Relationship Quality," *Journal of Personality and Social Psychology* 78, no. 2 (2000): 273–83.

6. Charles Gillis, "Psychiatrist George Valliant on Secrets to a Long Life and Bigger Salary," *Maclean's*, October 4, 2012, http://www2.macleans.ca/2012/10/04/the-secrets-to-a-long-life-and-a-bigger-salary-and-why-nice-guys-do-finish-first/.

7. Ladd Wheeler, Harry Reis, and John Nezlek, "Loneliness, Social Interaction and Social roles," *Journal of Personality and Social Psychology* 45, no. 4 (1983): 943–53. Reed W. Larson, "The Solitary Side of Life: An Examination of the Time People Spend Alone from Childhood to Old Age," *Developmental Review* 10, no. 2 (1990): 155–83.

8. Leaf Van Boven, "Experientialism, Materialism, and the Pursuit of Happiness," *Review of General Psychology* 9, no. 2 (2005): 132–42.

9. Sara Solnick and David Hemenway, "Is More Always Better? A Survey on Positional Concerns," *Journal of Economic Behavior and Organization* 37, no. 3 (1998): 373–83.

10. Leaf Van Boven and Thomas Gilovich, "To Do or to Have? That Is the Question," *Journal of Personality and Social Psychology* 85, no. 6 (2003): 1193–1202.

CHAPTER 5:

DREAM A DREAM

1. Ian Brissette, Michael F. Scheier, and Charles S. Carver, "The Role of Optimism and Social Network Development, Coping, and Psychological Adjustment during a Life Transition," *Journal of Personality and Social Psychology*, 82, no. 1 (2002): 102–11. Leslie P. Kamen and Martin E. P. Seligman, "Explanatory Style and Health," ed. M. Johnston and T. Marteau, in *Current Psychology* 6, no. 3 (1987): 207–18.

2. Simone Schnall et al., "Social Support and the Perception of Geographical Slant," *Journal of Experimental Social Psychology* 44, no. 5 (2008): 1246–55.

3. Dan Kadlec, "How a Digital Picture of Your Future Self Can Change Your Savings Habits," *Time*, February 29, 2012, http://business.time.com/2012/02/29/how-a-digital-picture-of-your-future-self-can-change-your-saving-habits/

4. Another report, *Behavioral Finance in Action* by Shlomo Benartzi at the UCLA Anderson School of Management, argues that it is extremely difficult for humans to envision themselves much older but that those who can conjure a realistic vision have a significantly higher savings rate.

5. Tali Sharot, *The Science of Optimism: Why We're Hard-Wired for Hope*, (TED conference, November 18, 2012, available from Amazon Digital Services).

6. Daniel Kahneman, "Objective Happiness" in *Well-Being: The Foundations of Hedonic Psychology*, ed. Daniel Kahneman, Edward Diener, and Norbert Schwarz (New York: Russell Sage Foundation), 3–25.

7. Roy F. Baumeister, "Self-and Identity: A Brief Overview of What They Are, What They Do, and How They Work," *Annals of the New York Academy of Sciences* 1234 (October 2011): 48–55.

8. James 4:14.

9. Ecclesiastes 1:2 HCSB.

10. Romans 5:5.

11. Hebrews 11:1.

12. Carla J. Berg, C. R. Snyder and Nancy Hamilton, "The Effectiveness of a Hope Intervention in Coping with Cold Pressor Pain," *Journal of Health Psychology* 13, no. 6 (2008): 804–9.

13. Ethan Hale, "Goals: The Difference between Success and Failure," *Fast Company*, December 5, 2011, http://www.fastcompany.com/1798754/goals-difference-between-success-and-failure.

14. Utaka Komura et al., "Responses of Pulvinar Neurons Reflect a Subject's Confidence in Visual Categorization," *Nature Neuroscience* 393 (June 2013): 393.

15. Jennifer Sullivan, "Woman Who Refused to Sell Tiny Ballard Home Dies, *Seattle Times*, June 17, 2008, http://seattletimes.nwsource.com/html/local-news/2008002522_webedithobit17m.html.

CHAPTER 6:

CELEBRATE EACH OTHER

1. Shelly Gable and Jonathan Haidt, "What (and Why) Is Positive Psychology?" *Review of General Psychology* 9, no. 2 (2005): 103–10.

2. Natalya Maisel and Shelly L. Gable, "The Paradox of Received Social Support: The Importance of Responsiveness," *Psychological Science* 20, no. 8 (2009): 928–32.

3. This chart is adapted from the work of Shelly L. Gable et al., "What Do You Do When Things Go Right? The Interpersonal and Intrapersonal Benefits of Sharing Positive Events," *Journal of Personality and Social Psychology* 87, no. 2 (2004): 228–45; and Carol Dweck, *Mindset: The New Psychology of Success*, (New York: Random House, 2006).

4. Gable et al., "What Do You Do When Things Go Right?"

5. Anthony Scinta and Shelly Gable, "Automatic and Self-Reported Attitudes in Romantic Relationships," *Personality and Social Psychology Bulletin* 33, no. 7 (2007): 1008–22.

6. Shelly Gable and Joshua Poore, "Which Thoughts Count? Algorithms for Evaluating Satisfaction in Relationships," *Psychological Science* 19, no. 10 (2008): 1030–36.

7. Dorothy Foltz-Gray, "What Makes Us Happy?" *Prevention*, November 2011, http://www.prevention.com/mind-body/emotional-health/what-makes-us-happy?page=4.

8. Kathleen Deveny, "We're Not in the Mood," *Newsweek*, June 30, 2003, 43.

9. Rachael Rettner, "Generous Couples Have Happier Marriages," *Today*, December 8, 2011, http://www.today.com/id/45604220/ns/today-today_health/t/generous-couples-have-happier-marriages/#.UZHnipXIYdl.

10. Douglas E. Rosenau, *A Celebration of Sex*, rev. ed. (Nashville: Thomas Nelson, 2002).

11. Anne J. Blood and Robert J. Zatorre, "Intensely Pleasurable Responses to Music Correlate with Activity in Brain Regions Implicated in Reward and Emotion," *Proceedings of the Natural Academies of Sciences* 98, no. 20 (September 25, 2001).

12. Tom Horan, "Can Music Make Us Happy?" *Telegraph*, November 24, 2006, http://musicmagic.wordpress.com/2008/07/08/can-music-make-us-happy/.

13. Robin Lloyd, "Amazing Power of Music Revealed," *LiveScience*, October 15, 2008, http://www.livescience.com/2953-amazing-power-music-revealed.html.

14. Jeremy Hsu, "Music-Memory Connection Found in the Brain," *LiveScience*, February 24, 2009, http://www.livescience.com/5327-music-memory-connection-brain.html.

15. Kira Birditt, Susannah Hope, Edna Brown, and Terri Orbuch, "Developmental Trajectories of Marital Happiness Over 16 Years," *Research in Human Development* 9, vol. 2 (2012): 126–44.

16. Tara Parker-Pope, "The Generous Marriage," *New York Times Magazine*, December 11, 2011, http://well.blogs.nytimes.com/2011/12/08/is-generosity-better-than-sex/.

CHAPTER 7:
ATTUNE YOUR SPIRITS

1. "The Engagement." *Seinfeld.* Directed by Andy Ackerman, written by Larry David. NBC. Season 7, Episode 111, air date September 21, 1995.

2. David H. Olson and Amy K. Olson, *Empowering Couples: Building on Your Strengths* (Minneapolis: Life Innovations, 2000).

3. Robert J. Sternberg, "Triangulating Love," in *The Altruism Reader: Selections from Writings on Love, Religion, and Science,* ed. Thomas Oord (West Conshohocken, PA: Templeton Press, 2007). Also Robert J. Sternberg, "A Triangular Theory of Love," in *Close Relationships*, ed. Harry T. Reis and Caryl E. Rusbult (New York: Psychology Press, 2004).

4. Daniel J. Hruschka, *Friendship: Development, Ecology, and Evolution of a Relationship* (Berkley, CA: University of California Press, 2010).

5. Christopher R. Agnew et al., "Cognitive Interdependence: Commitment and the Mental Representation of Close Relationships," *Journal of Personality and Social Psychology* 74, no. 4 (1998): 939–54.

6. J. P Laurenceau et al., "Intimacy as an Interpersonal Process: Current Status and Future directions," in *Handbook of Closeness and Intimacy*, ed. Debra J. Mashek and Arthur Aron (Mahwah, NJ: Erlbaum, 2004), 61–78.

7. K J. Prager and L. J Roberts, "Deep Intimate Connections: Self and Intimacy in Couple Relationships," in Ibid., 43–60.

8. Daniel Akst "America: Land of Loners?" *The Wilson Quarterly*, Summer 2010, http://www.wilsonquarterly.com/article.cfm?AID=1631.

9. Lisa A. Neff and Benjamin R. Karney, "The Dynamic Structure of Relationship Perceptions: Differential Importance as a Strategy of Relationship Maintenance," *Personality and Social Psychology Bulletin* 29, no. 11 (2003): 1433–46.

10. John Bowlby, *Loss: Sadness and Depression* vol. 3 of *Attachment and Loss*, ed. John Bowlby (New York: Basic Books, 1982).

11. Jeffrey Kluger, "The Biology of Belief," *Time,* February 12, 2009.

12. An increasing amount of scientific research is focusing on the relationship between religion and mental health. *Time* magazine reported some of the findings. Religious people are less depressed, less anxious, and less suicidal than nonreligious

people, and they are better able to cope with such crises as illness and bereavement. Even if you compare two people who have symptoms of depression, says Michael McCullough, an associate professor of psychology and religious studies at the University of Miami, "the more religious person will be a little less sad."

13. Pamela Paul, "The Power of Uplift," *Time,* January 17, 2005.

14. Patricia Murphy of Rush University Medical Center in Chicago concluded a study she conducted on improved response to medical treatment by saying: "In our study, the positive response to medication had little to do with the feelings of hope that typically accompanies spiritual belief. It was tied specifically to the belief that a Supreme Being cared." February 23, 2010, http://www.rush.edu/webapps/MEDREL/servlet/NewsRelease?id=1353. The ultimate feeling of intimacy—that God *cares* for you brings with it an inordinate amount of benefits, including a great deal of happiness.

15. David Lapp, "Marriage as Friendship," *Love and Fidelity Network* (program of the Collegiate Cultural Foundation), (2013), http://www.loveandfidelity.org/online_journal/marriage-as-friendship-by-david-lapp/.

16. Thomas N. Bradbury, Frank D. Fincham, and Steven R. H. Beach (2000), "Research on the Nature and Determinants of Marital Satisfaction: A Decade in Review," *Journal of Marriage and the Family* 62 (November 2000): 964–80.

17. John M. Gottman and Nan Silver, *The Seven Principles for Making Marriage Work* (New York: Crown Books, 1999), 19–20, 48.

18. Ibid.

19. Arthur Aron et al., "Couples Shared Participation in Novel and Arousing Activities and Experienced Relationship Quality," *Journal of Personality and Social Psychology* 78, no. 2 (2000): 273–83.

20. Valerian Derlega et al., "Developing Close Relationships," in *Self-Disclosure* (Newbury Park, CA: Sage Publications, 1993).

21. Benjamin R. Karney and Thomas N. Bradbury, "Attributions in Marriage: State or Trait? A Growth Curve Analysis," *Journal of Personality and Social Psychology* 78, no. 2 (2000): 295–309.

22. Benjamin Vima, *Prayerfully Yours: Quality Prayer for Quality Life* (Bloomington, IN: Trafford Publishing, 2012).

23. Lyubomirsky, *The How of Happiness: A New Approach to Getting the Life You Want.*

24. Margaret M. Poloma and George H. Gallup, *Varieties of Prayer: A Survey Report.* (Philadelphia: Trinity Press International, 1991).

25. C. S. Lewis, *Mere Christianity* (New York: Harper Collins, 1952), 50.

26. Forty-seven percent of people who report attending religious services several times a month describe themselves as "very happy," versus 28 percent of those who attend less than once a month. Kenneth I. Pargament and Annette Mahoney, "Spirituality: Discovering and Conserving the Sacred" in C. R. Snyder and Shane J. Lopez, eds., *Handbook of Positive Psychology*, 646–59.

27. According to the study, 70 percent of husbands who attend church regularly say they are "very happy" in their marriages, compared to only 59 percent of husbands who do not attend religious services. For women, the figures were similar, with a majority of those who attend church services reporting to be happier than those who do not. Read more at http://www.christianpost.com/news/church-attendance-key-to-marriage-success-researcher-says-33079/#rlpGtwPGUx1zbE81.99.

28. "Church Attendance Beneficial to Marriage, Researchers Says," CNSnews.com, July 7, 2008, http://www.cnsnews.com/news/article/church- attendance-beneficial-marriage-researcher-says.

CHAPTER 8:
ADD VALUE TO OTHERS

1. Lyubomirsky, Sheldon, and Schkade, "Pursuing Happiness: The Architecture of Sustainable Change," 111–31.

2. Dietrich Bonhoeffer, "A Wedding Sermon from a Prison Cell, May 1943" in *Letters and Papers from* Prison (New York: Touchstone, 1997), 43.

3. Hebrews 10:24.

4. Atul Gawande, "The Checklist," *New Yorker,* December 10, 2007, http://www.newyorker.com/reporting/2007/12/10/071210fa_fact_gawande.

5. "The Power of Making Lists," January 15, 2012, JuneauEmpire.com, http://juneauempire.com/opinion/2012-01-15/power-making-lists#.Uazg4JXIYdk.

6. Lyubomirsky, Sheldon, and Schkade, "Pursuing Happiness: The Architecture of Sustainable Change," 111–31.

7. Bruce Wydick, "Want to Change the World? Sponsor a Child," *Christianity Today,* June 2013, http://www.christianitytoday.com/ct/2013/june/want-to-change-world-sponsor-child.html.

CHAPTER 9:

OVERCOMING THE BIGGEST HURDLES

TO HAPPINESS AS A COUPLE

1. Eric Aasen, "Dallas Police Department Dropping Police Code for Plain English," *Dallas Morning News*, March 23, 2009.

2. Ecclesiastes 3:4.

3. Stephanie Pappas, "Money Is at the Root of Unhappy Marriages," *LiveScience*, October 13, 2011, Mother Nature Network, http://www.mnn.com/family/family-activities/stories/money-is-at-the-root-of-unhappy-marriages.

4. Megan Garber, "Are Your Facebook Friends Stressing You Out? (Yes)," *Atlantic*, November 2012, http://www.theatlantic.com/technology/print/2012/11/are-your-facebook-friends-stressing-you-out-yes/265626/.

5. Alex Aciman, "The Pursuit of Happiness," *Time*, July 15, 2013, 32.

6. Proverbs 13:10 NLT.

7. Paula Szuchman and Jenny Anderson, *Spousonomics: Using Economics to Master Love, Marriage and Dirty Dishes* (New York: Random House, 2011), 46.

8. Annie Van Bergen, *Task Interruption* (Amsterdam: North-Holland Publishing, 1968).

9. Excerpted from Edgar A. Guest, "Tomorrow," *Collected Verse* (Cutchogue, NY: Buccaneer Books, 1994), 71–73. Used by permission.

10. A. Peter McGraw, Barbara A. Mellers, and Philip E. Tetlock, "Expectation and Emotions of Olympic Athletes," *Journal for Experimental Social Psychology* 41 (2005): 438–46.

11. Victoria Husted Medvec, Scott F. Madey, and Thomas Gilovich, "When Less Is More: Counterfactual Thinking and Satisfaction among Olympic Medalists," *Journal of Personality and Social Psychology* 69, no. 4 (1995): 603–10.

12. Daniel Gilbert, *"What You Don't Know Makes You Nervous,"* New York Times.com, May 21, 2009, http://www.wjh.harvard.edu/~dtg/WHAT%20YOU%20DONT%20KNOW%20MAKES%20YOU%20NERVOUS.pdf.

CHAPTER 10:
YOUR THREE-WEEK HAPPINESS PLAN

1. Lyubomirsky, *The How of Happiness: A Scientific Approach to Getting the Life You Want*, 62.

2. Alvaro Pascual-Leone et al., "Characterizing Brain Cortical Plasticity and Network Dynamics across the Age-span in Health and Disease with TMS-EEG and TMS-fMRI," *Brain Topography* 24, no. 3-4 (2011): 302–15.

3. Shawn Achor, "Positive Intelligence," *Harvard Business Review*, January-February 2012, http://hbr.org/2012/01/positive-intelligence/.

CONCLUSION:
HAPPILY EVER AFTER?

1. Sandra L. Murray, Dale W. Griffin, Jaye L. Derrick, Brianna Harris, Maya Aloni, and Sadie Leder "Tempting Fate or Inviting Happiness? Unrealistic Idealization Prevents the Decline of Marital Satisfaction," *Psychological Science* 22 (2011): 619–26.

2. Daniel J. Levinson, *Seasons of a Man's Life* (New York: Random House, 1978).

FIGHT★NIGHT
with DRS. LES & LESLIE PARROTT
"Drs. Les and Leslie are hilarious and we learned a ton!"
- Ranjy T, Portland
Conflict is the price we pay for a deeper level of intimacy.
Spend a fun-filled evening with Drs. Les and Leslie learning how conflict can bring you closer together. This live event is for everyone—regardless of age or stage.Find an event in your area or invite Drs. Les and Leslie to speak in your community: LesandLeslie.com

Find joy...
in helping a child

Les and Leslie Parrott are pleased to partner with World Vision to build a better world for children in need.

World Vision is a Christian humanitarian organization dedicated to working with children, families, and their communities worldwide to reach their full potential by tackling the causes of poverty and injustice.

Sponsor a child today!

To learn how you can experience the joy of changing lives and find a child to help, visit:

www.lesandleslie.com/worldvision

WORTHY
P U B L I S H I N G

IF YOU ENJOYED THIS BOOK, WILL YOU CONSIDER SHARING THE MESSAGE WITH OTHERS?

- Mention the book in a Facebook post, Twitter update, Pinterest pin, or blog post.

- Recommend this book to those in your small group, book club, workplace, and classes.

- Head over to facebook.com/lesandleslieparrott, "LIKE" the page, and post a comment as to what you enjoyed the most.

- Tweet "I recommend reading #makinghappy by @LesParrott // @worthypub"

- Pick up a copy for someone you know who would be challenged and encouraged by this message.

- Write a book review online.

You can subscribe to Worthy Publishing's newsletter at worthypublishing.com.

**WORTHY PUBLISHING
FACEBOOK PAGE**

**WORTHY PUBLISHING
WEBSITE**